NATIONAL GEOGRAPHIC DIRECTIONS

Desert Memories

ARIEL DORFMAN

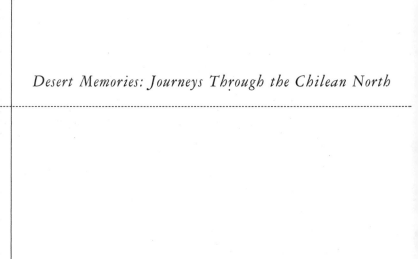

Desert Memories: Journeys Through the Chilean North

NATIONAL GEOGRAPHIC DIRECTIONS

NATIONAL GEOGRAPHIC
Washington, D.C.

Published by the National Geographic Society
1145 17th Street, N.W., Washington, DC 20036-4688

Library of Congress Cataloging-in-Publication Data

Dorfman, Ariel.
    Desert memories : journeys through the Chilean North / Ariel Dorfman.
        p. cm. -- (National Geographic directions)
    ISBN 0-7922-6240-9
    1. Norte Grande Region (chile)--Description and travel. 2. Dorfman,
Ariel--Travel--Chile--Norte Grande Region. I. Title. II. Series.

F3205.D67 2003
918.3'1--dc22

                                                                2003058825

One of the world's largest nonprofit scientific and educational organizations, the National Geographic Society was founded in 1888 "for the increase and diffusion of geographic knowledge." Fulfilling this mission, the Society educates and inspires millions every day through its magazines, books, television programs, videos, maps and atlases, research grants, the National Geographic Bee, teacher workshops, and innovative classroom materials. The Society is supported through membership dues, charitable gifts, and income from the sale of its educational products. This support is vital to National Geographic's mission to increase global understanding and promote conservation of our planet through exploration, research, and education.

For more information, please call 1-800-NGS LINE (647-5463), write to the Society at the above address, or visit the Society's Web site at www.nationalgeographic.com.

Interior design by Michael Ian Kaye and Tuan Ching, Ogilvy & Mather, Brand Integration Group

Printed in the U.S.A.

This book is for Angélica, my co-pilot and navegante *in this and all the other deserts.*

CONTENTS

Desert Memories

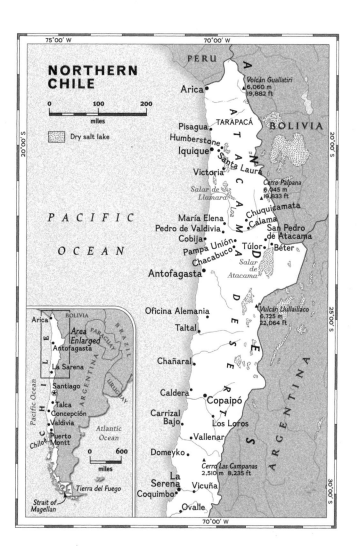

NORTHERN CHILE

0   100   200
miles

Dry salt lake

PERU

Arica

Volcán Guallatiri
6,060 m
19,882 ft

Pisagua
Humberstone
Iquique
Santa Laura
Victoria

TARAPACÁ

BOLIVIA

Cerro Palpana
6,045 m
19,833 ft

Salar de
Llamara

María Elena
Pedro de Valdivia
Cobija
Pampa Unión
Chacabuco

Chuquicamata
Calama
San Pedro
de Atacama
Túlor • Béter

Salar
de
Atacama

Antofagasta

PACIFIC

OCEAN

A T A C A M A

D E S E R T

A N D E S

Oficina Alemania

Taltal

Vulcán Llullaillaco
6,725 m
22,064 ft

Chañaral

Caldera
Copaipó
Carrizal
Bajo
Los Loros
Vallenar

Domeyko

Cerro Las Campanas
2,510 m 8,235 ft

La
Serena
Coquimbo

Vicuña

Ovalle

ARGENTINA

BOLIVIA

Arica

Area
Enlarged

Antofagasta

La Sarena

PARAGUAY

BRAZIL

Pacific Ocean

C H I L E

Santiago

Talca
Concepción
Valdivia
Puerto
Montt

Chiloé

URUGUAY

ARGENTINA

Atlantic
Ocean

0   600
miles

Tierra del Fuego

Strait of
Magellan

PROLOGUE

Opening in Arica: Circling Back

Monday, May 27, 2002.

So this is where my journey ends, here where my country ends and where the desert ends, here in Arica, this port at the north-ernmost tip of Chile. This is the moment, as my plane lifts up into the air to fly to Santiago, this is when the three-week road trip that Angélica and I have just taken through el Norte Grande, the Chilean North, will begin to recede into the past and start to become a memory, a memory of ours and perhaps also a memory of the desert down there below that stretches for numberless miles southward from Arica and that seems to remember everything that ever happened to it, remembers and eventually destroys everything that happens to it.

I had been in Arica before and crossed that same desert forty years ago without having left a mark on it, almost without letting it touch me. Arica—where the South American continent begins to widen and expand to the west, inaugurating what is called *la cintura cósmica de América,* the cosmic waist of America—had been the only city in the North of Chile that I'd slept in, if only for a night. At that point in my life, a twenty-year-old convert to the cause of *América Latina,* I had no time for the ghost towns of the nitrate boom and bust, I did not stop to see the largest open-pit copper mine in the world at Chuquicamata, I was not interested in the colonial white adobe village of San Pedro de Atacama, which had been the central oasis in the route of the Inca, and—fool that I was—the magical port of Iquique was not in my plans. No, I was on my way to Lima and Cuzco and Machu Picchu, to Lake Titicaca and La Paz and Oruro, what I understood then as the hidden heart of the South American continent.

Born in Buenos Aires and then brought up in New York from ages two to twelve, I had defined myself upon my family's arrival in Chile in 1954 as an American kid, absolutely urban and resolutely monolingual in English. If I dreamt of any desert at all—mostly I dreamt, even in faraway Santiago, about the Yankees winning the pennant—it would have been one of those Hollywood deserts with fistfights in tinsel saloons and cacti and buzzards speckling a sun-baked waste in Arizona, unable to understand, at that point of my impoverished linguistic existence, how crucial the Spanish I did not wish to speak had been in the creation of that West I was conjuring up.

It had taken me many years of submerging myself in Chile to fall in love with the language and the continent I had repudiated as a child, and it was not the Norte Grande that I wanted to explore once I decided to reinvent myself as a Spanish speaker and a Latin American patriot. That hitchhiking trip back in 1962 was planned as a way in which to make up for lost time, spend an entire summer seeking out the great originating Inca and Tiawanaku civilizations that lay at the source of an Amerindian identity—all the rage in the sixties—that I had been determined to call my own.

Many years would pass before I realized that the barren surfaces I had skimmed over in the North of Chile in 1962 held many more secrets about the destiny I had picked for myself than all the ruins and canyons of the Andean highlands, no matter how wonderful they might be. My blindness, at that early date, to the pleasures and challenges of the Norte Grande should not be attributed solely to my immature search for roots where they did not exist, but also to a deep-seated prejudice against deserts in general, a prejudice which I admit only really started to be dispelled during this 2002 trip that has just come to its conclusion.

There was nothing there, I thought to myself automatically, back in 1962. Give me trees, give me greenery by the sea, give me forests next to a lake, give me a shaded valley where people feel immediately at home. I understood the attraction that a land with no vegetation and no animal life and no roads might hold for people, but it was a merely intellectual understanding and did not engage my guts, my most intimate affections. Perhaps I was afraid of precisely what so many others through history have found attractive in the emptiness: the solitude and extreme introspection that a landscape devoid of human habitation will force you to face with a vengeance, a truth about yourself that you can find nowhere else—which may be why so many of the great monotheistic religions have been bred in the wild. Or maybe I was merely wary of what the brutal and unforgiving light of those places might reveal about humanity, devils and saints seeking out the desert as their abode for a reason: because there are no shadows to hide behind. The desert, a place of death and testing, I thought, a place to avoid.

And yet, when I had been given a choice—what is the one locality, region, space in the world you want to visit?—I had selected the Norte Grande of Chile, the driest desert of them all.

Not an exaggeration.

Less rain falls on these sands than on any other similarly blighted expanse on Earth. I talked to men born in Arica, a woman brought up in Pisagua, men and women who had never ventured forth from the nitrate town of María Elena or never left the oasis of Pica, which produces the most fragrant oranges your tongue has ever rolled over, and none of them had felt one drop of rain on their bodies in their lives. And talking of bodies, in the Arica my plane was now leaving I had sniffed bodies thousands of years old, mummified by the hot sand of the desert, with the skin still stretched across the bridge of the nose and the lips parched dry and the face almost recognizable. One night in a bar in Iquique I heard about a certain university professor, Quinteros by name, who had decided to find a grandfather of his who had been buried in the cemetery adjoining an abandoned nitrate settlement in the middle of the Pampa del Tamarugal. After several days of research and excavations, Quinteros came upon a corpse that had to belong to the father of his father. No name was on the cross, but it was as if

Quinteros were looking, he said, at himself in the mirror. The beard, the teeth, the nose … all identical. So he took the old man in his arms as if he were a baby, caressed him, and carted him back to Iquique for reburial. Who needs DNA when you have the desert?

Oh yes, it rained once, some years ago, in the sprawling port of Antofagasta. Two millimeters. And several residents had died in the ensuing mudslide. By one of those freakish accidents that delights travelers and confounds natives, when Angélica and I were seventy miles from Antofagasta, passing ocher hills and pink brimstone and pulverized stone so pitiless they would put Hell to shame (because Hell at least has inhabitants), we were immersed in an altogether abnormal phenomenon, a sort of slight fog drizzling on our car. That semi-sprinkle had not reached Antofagasta itself, though there was an unusual front of turbulence sweeping in from the sea, so the reporter on the local radio was already trying to calm down a populace that had begun to panic, a woman had called in to say—much to our cruel mirth—that she thought she had felt a drop of rain fall upon her cheek and what should she do, should she evacuate her children?

To explain this exceptional lack of wet weather, all I have to do is look out the window of my plane. There is the main culprit: the Andes that I view through the zoom of my camera rising a few hundred miles off to the east, where Bolivia begins with its *mesetas* and its volcanoes, those supposedly immobile mountains that are being imperceptibly thrust upward with quiet violence. Since the end of the Jurassic period (in other words, for the last couple of hundred million years, a piddling amount of time in geological and cosmic terms), the Pacific tectonic plate, many miles down under the boundless waters of the ocean, has been ramming up against the South American plate and lifting the immense mountain range up and up, a couple of inches a year. It is those young mountains that do not allow the humidity that accumulates on their eastern side to pass through to the west. And from the west, any precipitation storming in from the widest expanse of water in the world is blocked and sponged up by the cold Peru Current of the Pacific that flows north from Antarctica.

Only one river in the whole thousand kilometers of desert, the Loa, its waters polluted with arsenic from the upstream copper mines, has the strength to dribble into the sea. All the other waterways that come tumbling down from the snow-capped heights into the gorges and onto the barren plains end up sucked underground, absorbed by the sand and the stone before reaching the Pacific. Until Arica, which welcomes two rivers, the Azapa and the Lluta, whose wide and fertile hundred-mile-long valleys I can see meeting just beneath my plane. Also underneath me, towering over the beaches of the city itself, is the large hill called El Morro de Arica, the last remnant and culmination of the *cordillera de la costa,* which ascends massively to the south, hugging the seashore for many hundreds of miles. A monumental seacoast mountain range that isolates the rest of the land from the sea and then falls abruptly into the Pacific, its final forbidding cliffs carved out of the rock by the wind and the erosion of time. Those abrupt ledges nearly a kilometer high make the narrow strips of soil, coves, and inlets where most of the inhabitants of the Norte Grande have had to live in order to survive almost inaccessible by land. It is that vast space between the cordillera de la costa and the cordillera de los Andes that Angélica and I have endlessly driven through in the last weeks, a broad basin or depression hemmed in by the two parallel barriers of mountains, and that from the air looks even more daunting than it did from a highway that at least offered us, with its pavement and its markers, a semblance of civilization.

And yet it had been to this Chilean desert that I had finally turned when I was given the opportunity to travel wherever I wanted, the very desert I had rushed through back in 1962. It had slowly colonized my mind, emerged ever more mythically inside me like an obsessive mist of sand, calling me to come and see for myself the territory that had decided the fate of the country I had made my own, the territory that had decided in many ways my own fate.

What a paradox: This desert that did not even belong to Chile for most of its existence, that had been wrested from Peru and Bolivia in a war in the late nineteenth century, had turned out to be the central determining factor in my nation's contemporary history. The land that would be called Chile was known—even before the Spanish conquistadors set their wary eyes and greedy hands upon it—as the end of the world, with the forbidding archipelagos of Tierra del Fuego and the icy expanse of Antarctica to the south, the endless Pacific Ocean where Robinson Crusoe (Alexander Selkirk, in fact) would one day be shipwrecked to the west, and the towering mass of the Andes to the east. And isolated to the north by the *desierto* now flowing beneath my plane, the expanse that the first Spanish chroniclers called the *despoblado de Atacama*—falsely suggesting it was uninhabited and uninhabitable—and that three hundred years later Charles Darwin, during his 1832 visit, would describe as a "complete and utter desert." Even that scientist who was fascinated with the slightest hint of vegetation that sprouted in his path and inspected every faint stirring of life, even he could find nothing redeeming in this emptiness. Pivotal, therefore, in the development of Chile because its mere desolation brooding to the north had circumscribed the country as an island, its lush Central Valley farmlands and southern forests a remote backwater in the eyes and ears of whatever empire happened to be on the rise, whether Incan, Spanish, or British.

It was not true, of course, that the desert had no inhabitants. I now knew that those coasts I saw down there as the airplane headed southward had been the home of the *changos* for thousands of years, and many of its gorges and oases had been colonized by other indigenous settlers, not to mention a subdued riot of wildlife, animals and brush, birds and bracken and insects. The desert, however, only developed into a fully active part of the modern destiny of Chile—and of the world—when nitrate made its appearance.

As long as there were human beings nearby—at least for ten thousand years—the desert had been mined for its other minerals, silver and iron and copper, enticing a few hardy men to eke out a living on its edges, but it was the discovery of boundless fields of what is known as saltpeter, existing nowhere else in the world in that natural state, its thousands of acres of crust out there for the taking, that changed the way the desert was perceived and also transformed it into the primary engine of Chile's progress as a nation. For forty-odd years Europe and the United States were to become as addicted to nitrate as Chile was, but for opposite reasons. That fiery mineral-salt had been valued for its use as gunpowder in the pre-Columbian era as well as for mining purposes throughout the Spanish colonial age, but what thrust it onto the global stage was its role as a miraculous, unequaled fertilizer at a time when the industrial revolution demanded a higher yield from the increasingly depleted fields and orchards that were supposed to feed the burgeoning urban populations of the United States and Europe. And that same industrial revolution was simultaneously creating the science that allowed the extraction of those white crystals on a mammoth scale, a series of technological advances that would conquer and colonize a desert that had, up till then, been too barren and unfriendly to allow permanent contemporary human settlement. Now, in places where not even a scorpion had dared to crawl, whole towns sprouted, complete with theaters visited by the leading companies of Europe and ballrooms where damsels sporting the latest fashions designed in Paris and manufactured in Manchester danced away the nights to the beat of live orchestras. And bays that had for millennia scarcely been able to offer much more than mussels to its unclad dwellers received tens of thousands of migrants from every corner of the world—China and Croatia, Athens and Cochabamba, Arequipa and Glasgow—while a hundred clippers a day waited to load the feverish white gold that trains incessantly brought to the shore, more railroad tracks built in one year over that parched earth than could be found in the rest of Latin America combined. Replenishing—until the nitrate bust of the

1920s—the stomachs and pocketbooks and stock exchanges of the Western powers.

And providing the Chilean state for almost fifty years with over half its revenue—the enclaves of modernity in the North (inhabited by less than 5 percent of the population) generating to its south a land with plenty of mansions and plenty of oligarchs and no taxes. No taxes, but also no need to address the terrible inequalities inherited from colonial times, no need to reform the old rural system that shackled the economy, no need to develop industry, no need to devise any truly participatory institutions of the kind that should accompany modernization. It fell to others to demand those changes in a society that kept the great majority of its people destitute and ignorant and voiceless—and the needs and ideas and organization of these others had, in fact, been born primarily in those very same nitrate mines whose workers had fathered the first Chilean democratic and socialist movements, the first social groups and trade unions in Latin America, which, even before the Mexican Revolution, had mapped out a strategy to bring freedom and justice and national autonomy to its citizens.

That desert, therefore, had engendered contemporary Chile, everything that was good about it, everything that was dreadful. The Chile of inequality and misery I witnessed as an adolescent, the Chile that gave me hope when I matured into a young man, that such inequities could be overcome with political struggle. The desert was at the source of the world I inhabited, even if I had not been ready to stop and see it during my first hasty visit.

I probably began to dimly understand this in the years that followed my return from that 1962 road trip, as I became involved in the liberation process headed by Salvador Allende, who in 1970 was to become the world's first socialist president elected in free elections. In a sense—even if I was only to realize this in retrospect—my own interest in the Norte Grande followed the trajectory of Allende himself, who, though born in Valparaíso, in Chile's región central, had ended up later in life as a senator representing the region of Tarapacá in the north of the country. In fact, every major ground-breaking political figure of the Chilean twentieth century, Alessandri and Frei and Recabarren, had all passed through the Norte Grande and been nurtured there. And Pinochet, yes, General Augusto Pinochet, who overthrew Allende in 1973 and was dictator of Chile until 1990, he had also spent many years commanding different posts in the North.

Strange that it should be Pinochet—who did not even know of my existence and couldn't have cared less—who would in a roundabout way keep me from the Norte Grande. Not that I am crazy enough to blame him directly. But I couldn't very well explore the North when I wasn't even allowed back anywhere in my own country for the first ten years of my exile, nor was such a trip conceivable once I tentatively began to return to Chile in mid-dictatorship or during the difficult years of transition to democracy that followed. I would watch that enigmatic territory, however, from the plane—as I do right now, at the end of this 2002 trip—each time I flew back and forth from the United States, promising myself as I watched its mountains and wild coast and sandblasted expanses below me, that someday I would have to really visit the desert I had missed so many years ago. A voyage to the origins, I murmured to myself, to a place where the modern world was born, where contemporary Chile had been spawned, where the quest for a better society had been first proposed as a task for the outcasts of Latin America. And a chance to face my own prejudice against deserts, against the lonely questions about death and survival that deserts ask us, a chance to discover what is left of the past, if it is swallowed by the sand and the heat or if it is preserved like the mummies of Arica.

But there were other motives—of a more personal and indeed carnal nature—for wanting to head into the desert, responsibilities, let us call them, that I had been accumulating through the years, that made the Norte Grande particularly resonant, particularly tempting. Another sort of past—and perhaps a debt that needed to be repaid—awaiting me in the desert.

In late 1973, a few months after the coup that had terminated the Allende experiment, Freddy Taberna, one of my pals from university days, had been executed by a firing squad in a desolate port called Pisagua, which I can, in fact, now see hugging the coastline as if it were about to sink into the sea, down there, right below the plane as it continues advancing toward Santiago.

That time when I first met Freddy in the early sixties had been a militant era, when students were at the forefront of a quest for a more equitable social order and true economic and cultural independence for our country and our continent, and Freddy's fearlessness in incessant skirmishes and confrontations with the police had brought him to my attention—and to everybody else's in the university, la Universidad de Chile. We partook of a few philosophy and history courses, but our real brotherhood was born in the gardens of the *Pedagógico,* where we patched together fervent plans for the liberation of everything oppressed in the universe.

We also shared a sense of humor, a mania for dancing to rock-and-roll and an obsession with recent Latin American culture, but what may have drawn us most to each other was that we hailed from opposite ends of the social spectrum. Whereas I was the son of a highly influential UN economist living in an ample house with two servants and an imported car at my disposal, Freddy—an illegitimate child—had been brought up in the mean streets of Iquique by his mother's brothers, all of them fishermen scratching out a day-to-day existence. One of the first things I noticed about Freddy— besides what I took to be his gaunt indigenous face—were his *alpargatas,* a sort of soft cloth slipperlike shoe. I never saw him wear anything else. It was almost as if he wished to flaunt his insolvency, fiercely show off his origins—and he managed, without hurting me, to rib me gently about the fact that I kept on trying to hide what I was, where I came from. In my search to become totally Latin American—the reason for my trip to Bolivia and Peru in 1962—he occupied a special, legendary place: someone who knew about the wretchedness we were trying to abolish, who came from that part of the continent, submerged, proud, autonomous, that I wanted so desperately to connect with and to which I suspected I could never fully belong. He was the first student I knew who lived in a university dorm—available in Chile only to the neediest scholarship students—and I may well have been the most cosmopolitan of his friends, and the abyss of privilege that yawned between us only increased our curiosity about each other, a mutual respect that was bolstered by the way in which I managed his campaign for the hotly contested and politically crucial post of president of our Student Union, using Madison Avenue slogans and marketing techniques, cartoons and competitions and jingles. We bonded deeply during those intense months that led to what can be considered in retrospect a turning point in university politics, when the revolutionary forces scored a historic victory. After graduating, we saw less of each other. He went off to Texas on a one-year visit, I was a visiting scholar at the University of California at Berkeley—both of us journeying to the land that we blamed for Chile's underdeveloped plight! When I returned to teach at the university, I heard he'd headed north to his native Iquique with his recent wife, Jinny—but we had always kept tabs on each other through friends, Luis Alvarado, Ricardo Nuñez, Isabel Allende (our future president's daughter). And his murder in the derelict concentration camp at Pisagua after the coup—which I read about in the Argentine Embassy, where I had found refuge—came to symbolize for me, perhaps more than the loss of any other friend, the destruction of the country, the pillaging of my past. The fact that his body had not been given back to his wife, that Freddy had become one of Chile's *desaparecidos,* may have been one of the reasons I have always felt so personally the drama of those missing men and women, kidnapped in life and still kidnapped in death by the military.

It would be ten years or so before I heard the details of how Freddy had died. I was in Toronto, doing a literary reading at Harbourfront, and Jinny, who had been given political

Calama: The author at the shrine of stones honoring the desaparecidos

asylum in Canada with her two now fatherless children, had sought me out and, over three long, painful hours, poured her story into my ears and my heart. We have to find him, she said as our encounter was coming to its end—we are going to find him. *Lo vamos a encontrar.*

But his body never appeared. Not when democracy returned, not when excavations were ordered by a judge, not when the army began—after Pinochet's arrest in London in

1998—to reluctantly release some information about where other remains may have been buried.

When I had planned this trip north, I was very aware that I would pass through the Iquique where Freddy had been born and where he had been arrested and where his friends and family still remembered him, very mindful that it was only a slight detour off the main road to visit Pisagua, where he had been executed and ... maybe it was time to find him, I had said to myself as Angélica and I started out on our voyage three weeks ago, maybe I will find traces of my old friend again.

But Freddy was not the only dead person we were looking for. There were others awaiting our visit.

Angélica's family on her father's side had come from Iquique, both her Malinarich grandfather and her Müller grandmother. But due to a family falling-out, Angélica had been cut off from that branch of her past for a good part of her life. Only rumors and legends had come down to her over the years, leaving her a muddled trail of stories about her lineage that we expected to clear up on this visit to the Norte Grande upon which those ancestors—from Croatia? from Greece? from Peru? from Germany?—had descended over a century ago as part of the nitrate rush. There were tales of fortunes amassed and fortunes squandered, tales of pirates and slaves and buried treasure, tales of a despondent woman walking into the sea because she could not marry her lover, tales of a grandfather who had abandoned his pregnant wife to run off with his sister-in-law, a genealogy of mysteries and question marks. In nearly a century, not one member of Angélica's immediate family had returned to Iquique to find out what truth, if any, was concealed in these stories.

Angélica's origins—and therefore the origins of our children and grandchildren—were entangled with the origins of the North of Chile, part and parcel of the story of how everyday people had loved and lived through the extraordinary experiment of conquering a desert.

Following in their footsteps, trying to wrest from the sands and ghost towns and survivors the secrets of an ever retreating past.

That was the multiple quest that was ending today along with the desert and its memories as the plane flew south to Santiago.

Santiago.

Where, the pilot informs the passengers, it is raining cats and dogs.

FIRST PART: ORIGINS

Footprint in the South

Wednesday, May 8, 2002. Valdivia/Puerto Montt.

I am standing with a box in my hands in a windowless storage area unobtrusively hidden among the classrooms and offices of the campus of the Universidad Austral here in Valdivia, a box that I hold gingerly, because inside it is the oldest footprint in the Americas, inside this box is the one trace left behind by a child who walked these lands 12,500 years ago. Or maybe it was thirteen thousand years ago. We cannot know. What has been scientifically verified is that at a certain moment many millennia ago, in the site now called Monte Verde—a marshy field around one hundred and eighty kilometers to the south of where my own feet now stand—a small mortal foot stepped very firmly in the mud and ashes next to a hearth where his family had been cooking one of their meals. Or is it her family, was that child female? If I could open this very ordinary-looking cardboard box—tightly closed, crisscrossed with black duct tape, its contents sealed away behind brownish wrapping paper—what I might see under the dusty fluorescent bulb is *la huella,* as it is called in Spanish, I could see the clear imprint of five toes and the outline of what might have been some sort of thin sandal or footwear, the silhouette of the heel. An ordinary footprint created when an ordinary leg just like any one of the many billion legs that have trudged across this Earth of ours briefly pressed down into clay and then was lifted up and then was gone. Two other marks that might possibly be construed as footprints were found upstream at the same site, but the huella is the only one of the three that is entirely and unmistakably a tread made by a person, one more spectacular bit of evidence to join the thousands of other residues of habitation rescued from Monte Verde that prove that humans had, so far back in time, already established an extremely sophisticated settlement in the Americas.

The truth is, I had not expected the huella to be deposited in such unpretentious surroundings or safeguarded inside this one box among several dozen other similar containers holding artifacts and utensils made from burnt wood and carved from the tusks of mastodons, cordage and residues of cloth and herbs and all sorts of other Pleistocene remnants, the whole lot piled into an old cabinet and shoved against one of the ugly light green paneled walls. Accustomed to the glossy indirect lighting and slick atmosphere of museum displays, I had foreseen security locks and sentinels, bureaucratic procedures and protective devices. When I had inquired by mail if I would really be admitted into the presence of this anthropological treasure, Mario Pino Quivira, the geologist who is my host and who now smiles at the receptacle in my hands and also perhaps at my puzzlement, had written to me that the *"huella está bajo mil candados y llaves,"* the footprint was under a thousand locks and keys. But there was only one key to this small warehouse-like structure and it was hanging from a hook in a tiny cubicle at the entrance to this modest one-story building that houses the university's Institute of Geosciences. And faculty and students—and who knows who else—can freely visit and roam this storage room and take a peek at its other occupant, a ten-foot derrick-shaped Russian seismograph from 1908, the last such extant machine functioning in the world.

It may be oddly appropriate that the most ancient indication yet of a trail left by humanity in the Americas should be guarded, dragonlike, by this large machine designed to gauge the upheavals of the Earth's movements, because that footprint represents an archaeological earthquake unleashed by the discovery, almost seventeen years ago, of the Monte Verde materials stowed away in this ugly storage space, changing forever the way in which we currently understand the lives of America's first inhabitants.

The dethroning of the paradigm that had for fifty years dominated the interpretation of American prehistory had started in the most unassuming of places, a cow pasture crossed by the Chinchihuapi creek thirty rough road-kilometers west of the fishing town of Puerto Montt, a place that I had visited just yesterday, Tuesday, May 7. I had flown more than a thousand kilometers south from Santiago, eager to again visit a Puerto

Montt that I had often used as a base for my many past explorations of the profusely forested Sur Chileno, my favorite sort of landscape, with rushing rivers green as emeralds and smoking volcanoes, and the sea, the wildest sea imaginable, as the South American continent on its Pacific side disintegrates into a turbulent excess of archipelagos, broken islands, and glaciers on its way to the Strait of Magellan. No time for any of that when I landed, as Monte Verde was in my sights and I needed to hurry before an announced downpour would make it even more difficult to reach the out-of-the-way site. Though the rain bogging me down would not have been an anomalous experience: The area around Puerto Montt is, after all, one of the most damp and drenched places in Chile.

Wait! Wait a second!

Wasn't I supposed to be going to the desert? Wasn't the grand plan for me to be challenged by the dry treeless solitude? What right did I have to feast my eyes once again on the magnificent delta of the Valdivia River flowing relentlessly toward the sea in the midst of a plethora of foliage, wander through the lovely botanical gardens on the island that harbors the campus of the Universidad Austral? Wasn't this a trip to the Norte Grande?

Contradictions that Angélica, who refused to come along for an absurd two-day dash to the Sur Chileno before driving north from Santiago into the sands of the Atacama, had not been reluctant to point out. But I convinced myself, if not her. This Chilean journey was to the origins, right, the origins of just about everything that I cared about—so what could be more pertinent than to kick it off from the oldest human habitation in the Americas, the place where it had all begun?

To reach that far south, hadn't the ancestors of the men and women of Monte Verde passed through the desert, hadn't those forefathers and foremothers been the first humans to see the desert where we were heading, the first ones to suffer its sands and give them a name?

And so I had found myself guided yesterday to that rainy field by Eduardo Alvar, a gentle giant of a man who had studied forestry and conservation and was one of the directors of the foundation created by the discoverers of Monte Verde in order to protect the site and search for funds to build a museum in its vicinity.

It was the humbleness of the place that struck me, if the verb to strike were not too dramatic a word to use for a setting so unruffled and serene and that would have been silent if it had not been for the intermittent contented snorts of pigs on the other side of the barbed-wire fence that cut the meadow in two, one a swarthy black, the other disconcertingly pink. Such a picture of rural bliss, with its rolling grassy knolls and thickety trees and sandy pebble beach next to a brook. It was hard to imagine those ancestors of ours cooking their meals where cows now munched and lowed and flicked their tails while a flock of geese noisily crossed the pastures that thousands of years ago had seen the wild mastodon roam, an animal popularly confused with an elephant but in fact more like a giant tapir. Nothing to recall how precarious life had been back then. The only peril that one needed to avoid in the twenty-first century were the large slops of cow dung liberally strewn around the field.

Eduardo Alvar grinned at me: "You're a writer," he said. "Use your imagination. Over there was a swamp." I looked. He was gesturing toward a small hill overgrown with brush and a bramble of lichen-covered whitish trees. "We know because that's where some gigantic beast got stuck or maybe it went to die there. That's where the natives managed to kill it when it was immobilized or simply culled it, picked it apart once it had died. If it wasn't old or sick, humans back then would have been unable to hunt it down."

Use my imagination indeed: There weren't even signs of the excavations—pits five meters deep and often dozens of yards wide and long—that had turned this meadow into a major archaeological dig. The placid, quietly bubbling creek had changed its course, part of the embankment had crumbled, a bulldozer had filled in the holes, the grass had grown back again—nothing to remind a visitor of the feverish scientific activity that had been going on for almost a decade and had ceased only fifteen years ago, let alone recall the daily doings of those first Americans who had set up their *toldos*—tentlike huts—thirteen thousand years in the past.

A place so unexceptional that when members of the Barría family, owners of the property for several generations, had discovered some huge bones in late 1975 while widening the creek in order to haul dead trees to a nearby lumber mill, they considered the remains to be those of a rather colossal cow. Even so, the Barrías, homesteaders bordering poverty who spoke a mixture of Spanish and *chilote,* a dialect from the nearby island of Chiloé, and who did not have electricity, a phone, or running water in their ramshackle ranch house, decided to pass the relics on to the Universidad Austral de Valdivia where it was determined that they belonged to extinct megamammals. A year later, Professor Tom Dillehay, a U.S. archaeologist who was teaching at the university, confirmed that these remains and others subsequently dug out of the site showed evidence of human agency—in other words, that they had been used and shaped by humans for instrumental purposes—and in the years that followed, Monte Verde gradually started to reveal a series of startling truths. By 1983 a large residential area, with almost a dozen domestic structures and a communal hearth and brazier, were recovered by Dillehay, who had been joined by Mario Pino and other scientists—and measurements indicated that Monte Verde might be the oldest settlement ever discovered in the Americas.

Up till then the reigning explanation of American prehistory was the Clovis paradigm: a fifty-year-old thesis that declared that migratory waves of men and women had, with their characteristically fluted spear points, crossed the Bering Strait by land at the end of the Ice Age and scattered all over the North American continent 11,500 years ago and from there gone on to colonize all other lands in the New World. And now, along came this obscure Chilean site 7,500 miles farther south and dated 1,000 to 1,500 radiocarbon years older, making latecomers of the Clovis tribes discovered originally in New Mexico. And such a reversal of previous dogma did not even take into account the presence of a second site at Monte Verde that hinted at the strong possibility of human habitation as far back as thirty-three thousand years, both Monte Verde sites pushing back human arrival in the Americas to a date forty thousand or fifty thousand years ago. Opening the door to a revision of many other earlier sites that had been dismissed before because of what Mario Pino called the Clovis "orthodoxy police" and allowing a plethora of new and old speculations about multiple entries and landings and routes for the original settlement of the Americas to flourish.

The defenders of the Clovis hypothesis, Eduardo Alvar had told me yesterday in Monte Verde and Mario Pino confirms the story today in Valdivia, had offered fierce resistance, claiming the site had not been adequately protected from contamination, counterattacking with a virulence and fanaticism that would have surprised the peaceful original inhabitants of Monte Verde. But perhaps even more astonishing to them than this ferocious academic strife would have been how the issue was finally resolved. In 1997 an eccentric, philanthropically inclined Texas millionaire—Mario says his clothes were all spangled in gold and that instead of calling cards he handed out ten-dollar bills with his name on them—had decided to pay for a group of the world's most eminent paleontologists and archaeologists to visit this very room in Valdivia where I now stand with the huella in my hands and where Mario Pino informs me, amiably taking the box from me, that the foray by the twelve scientists had been the last occasion when this carton had been opened, the only time the footprint in its silicone cast had been extracted from its hiding place for prying eyes to examine since it had been bundled up many years ago. The experts—among them was my friend Lautaro Núñez, whom I will visit ten days from now in the northern oasis village of San Pedro de Atacama—had then gone on the next day to Puerto Montt to inspect the site itself and had ended the expedition by proposing a toast in a bar in nearby Pelluco to the death of the paradigm of Clovis.

"There's something that puzzles me," I say to Mario now, this Wednesday morning, as he begins to forage in a rectangular wooden casket for a mastodon tusk, one of the prize items in the Valdivia collection, which enabled the Monteverdinos to dig wild potatoes out from the earth. "How did any of this survive the humidity, why did it not simply rot away?"

I was recalling an anecdote Eduardo Alvar had recounted yesterday when I had mentioned my astonishment at the lack of even a trace of the nearby or distant past at Monte Verde, the fact that nobody trekking through this backcountry road would have a clue as to its significance. Could the past be swallowed so effortlessly?

Eduardo stroked his beard and pointed in the direction of a field on the other side of the lane. One day some years ago Tom Dillehay had invited all the families near Monte Verde to a *curanto* picnic. Curanto is a medley of seafood and vegetables simmered in an underground oven for hours that leaves in its delicious wake an untidy clutter of shells. Everyone was surprised that Dillehay, a meticulous man of spartan customs who hates waste and disorder, encouraged his guests to leave a mess behind. He'd then drawn a map of the trash, photographed each item, and proposed to come back periodically to see how much of the debris would be spared by natural erosion. Three years later, the vegetation had already covered all traces of the carousing picnickers. In another experiment, an almost identical replica of the sort of animal skin the Monteverdinos had used to clothe themselves was exposed to the weather and the fungi: Twenty years later it could not be recognized.

And yet, at times, something as delicate as a footprint

does miraculously manage to withstand almost thirteen thousand years of decay. It turns out that wetlands often preserve a record of the past more faithfully than dry land does. In Monte Verde, by sheer chance—and luck is the unsung heroine of most archaeological breakthroughs—natural seals had isolated the site from organic decomposition: a first layer of sand sediment and then another level of ferrous oxide, which eliminated oxygen and was impermeable to dampness, plus a lining of peat that did not allow the rain to percolate down.

And then there are hunches. With a little help from nature.

In this case, from a bird.

Eduardo Alvar had just suggested it might be time to try and visit the Barría house a few hundred yards away from the site and see if we could ferret out Checho Barría, who had been present as a child at the huella's discovery, but now a bird had come flying across the field and alighted on the other side of the embankment where we stood. A long silence ensued. The bird looked at us, hopped around, waited.

Repeating what a bird just like it had done, according to Eduardo, many years ago—probably in 1983 when the team had been excavating for a long time and had not hit on anything that could be called spectacular for a good while. It was a period where the digging followed what Tom Dillehay called a "gut feeling" strategy, combining intuition and experience. Every morning they'd wake up and the same routine question would come up. Where should we start today? There, here, over there. Not advancing much.

And every morning a bird—an *aguilucho,* a small eaglelike bird—kept on returning to the same spot, perching there calmly, cocking its head to one side, as if it were curious about the work of these strange intruders. Until one day Dillehay said, "OK, tell you what, let's dig where that bird keeps showing up."

Maybe the bird was a messenger from the origins. Maybe it was the only living witness that had remained, replicating itself from generation to generation, one bird giving birth to the next one over thirteen thousand years until someone came along to rescue the past. Because the place where the bird kept stubbornly alighting was where some days later the three footprints surfaced out of a bed of hardened mud—one of them perfect, faultless, the big toe, the curve of the rest of the foot, the small size, 123 centimeters long—very close to what was then the creek passing through. Afterward, the stream changed course, so that when I finally stood next to Checho Barría and he showed me where the huella had once been discovered, what he pointed at was the clear, almost crystal-like water burbling through on a darkened bed of brownish pebbles. Checho had been ten years old when they had found the footprint—the very age that, for some reason, I had automatically assigned to the child who so many millennia ago had made that imprint in the earth on his way to who knows what task.

Again, the team was lucky. An excruciatingly diligent young student, Doris López, had been working on that part of the site, using a brush of extra-fine hairs and a bamboo spatula to clear away the silt from a sort of flat hollow that lay near where one of the primitive toldos/tents had once been erected, and Mario remembers how she had suddenly asked a strange sort of question, *¿qué está pasando?*—what is happening?— because she had come across a different sort of material, soft, that would need, Mario thought, extreme patience not to be damaged. "If it hadn't been for her," Mario says, "*delicadísima,* superbly delicate those supersmooth fingers of hers, we'd have lost it."

And then, there it was, revealed for all of them to see, the first time in thirteen thousand years that human eyes had seen what that human foot had faintly left behind. Along with the immediate question: how to preserve it? "These things," Mario says to me in this storage room in Valdivia, "they're like … *un suspiro en el viento.* A sigh in the wind."

The team became quite desperate. Fortunately, it wasn't raining that day, but there was nothing in Puerto Montt that could be used to keep the footprint from deteriorating. No plastic, no polyester, certainly no silicone. They snapped photos—and then cut through the sediment, removed a whole square meter of earth and placed plaster underneath it and a special cloth on top and then covered it yet again with plaster. As if it were a baby. The oldest baby in the Americas.

And what had he felt, I asked Mario, when he'd seen it there, the huella?

"One thing is to see artifacts presumably made by somebody and another is to see the *pisada* someone made, what their foot left in the earth. That's what gives you the sense of humanity, right? Whoever it was seemed to be wearing a moccasin, not even in her bare feet."

A rainbow of emotions began to play in his voice.

Last night, at dinner, Mario Pino had told me about how he imagined those ancestors of ours to have lived. He may be a geologist with a doctorate from the University of Münster in

Westphalia, numbers and experiments and charts at his finger-tips, but I suspect that what fascinates him about his profession is the prospect of burrowing into the lives and minds of those human beings his science is measuring.

He told me how these men and women had selected the best possible spot for survival: where running water would allow them to escape danger at a moment's notice ("streams are like pathways," he said) as well as providing an endless supply of stones that could be forged into instruments. Always next to a forest—if there was no meat to scavenge, there would be berries, grains, an abundance of mushrooms. And this encampment had been either a permanent home or one that they returned to year after year, too much loving labor, long hours expended in shaping and hewing tree trunks for this to be a transitional locale. He told me about the advanced forms of technology the Montverdinos had at their disposal, their use of clay to isolate their hearth from the earth, clay that needed to be brought from somewhere else, oh so valuable clay that lets heat go upward, retains embers, deposits a bed of ashes into which a young human had stepped quite unawares so many myriad days and nights ago. And the knots—"there is nothing more human than a knot," Mario said—that allowed the cords holding the tent in place to tense or slacken with the wind. And the carpet inside the habitation made out of hundreds of pieces of mastodon skin. And the oval form of the tent. And the stains on the floor from spat-out wads of *boldo,* an herb prized for its medicinal qualities that I still brew every time I visit Chile and that, because it was not grown locally, the Monteverdinos would have had to transport from Talca, hundreds of kilometers to the north. And Argentine plants that they would have had to bring from across the cordillera or acquire through trade with other groups.

And then there is that other smaller human habitation, some thirty meters away from the main toldo where they all slept—that structure where only one person could fit, placed in an east/west direction indicating precise deliberation. An herbarium inside, full of residues of medicinal and edible plants, up to sixty different varieties.

"We haven't written this in the book," Mario said, referring to the two hefty, scrupulously researched volumes on Monte Verde that the Smithsonian published in 1989 and 1997—"because so far they are speculations, but there has to have been a shaman, an old man or an old woman with enormous power inside the community, who knew when to harvest, what to harvest. To decide to eat a plant takes time, it's slow. Think of the eyes that needed to know what is food and what might be death."

Mario Pino stopped speaking for a few moments, in this room on campus, just as he often had during dinner. Yesterday afternoon when I had met him, the first thing he said was that I had to forgive any weariness he might show: He had just heard about the death of a close friend and colleague in Germany and it was affecting him. So I wondered if his frequent lapses into silence over our meal could be attributed to memories of that friend of his who had died, apparently alone, on the other side of the world. It was possible, because the next day—in other words, today during our morning session with the huella and other implements salvaged from Monte Verde—Mario reveals himself to be less serious and reserved, becomes more cheerful, whistling to himself, humming little songs under his breath, smiling more easily. But last night our conversation had been a bit more solemn as it turned to the wisdom of the shaman, her deep knowledge of much more than botany.

We tried to imagine her, that woman who suddenly finds an unknown plant and she has to classify it according to previous lore—this one is a relative of that one, it looks like this other one, this other one causes this sort of effect. So she tastes it with the tip of her tongue and waits to see what happens, *do I feel something, I feel nothing,* and she increases the dose and she's tasting and trying, trying and tasting. For a plant to pass from a savage state to domestication, many years need to pass. "It's not like eating meat," Mario said. "To eat meat you need a stick, you grab a bow and arrow, or you find a dead animal, you make some fire—and dinner's ready. To know, to gather, fifty, sixty species in a forest, that's hard work."

Wisdom is hard work, I agree. So there must have been lots of conversation at night, transmitting knowledge in those long winters under the toldo, many a night chewing over herbs and chewing over words, the need to talk and compare what you know, what you need others to know before death takes you away. It happened at night, Mario Pino thinks, when the dawn took its time in coming and there was a warm hearth inside and rain pouring from the sky outside and plenty of hours to spare. Talk so the nights would not be so long, hurry the sun into coming up word by word.

"They must have had a good life," Mario had said as our own evening was drawing to a close, *"una vida muy buena."* He sees those winters as pleasant in spite of the rain and wind howling outside; he was almost nostalgic about the stories they must have told around the fire.

"And the children? The child who left that footprint?"

"I'll show you something tomorrow," Mario had promised.

And that is why now—after having shut away the box with the huella in its cupboard, along with all the other instruments he's been showing me—he takes me to another room where he sets up a slide machine.

The picture of an object flashes on the screen and stays there, fixed.

"Look," he says. "You see this *boleadora?* It's a top. Look at this groove in the middle. Made for a child."

He tells me about a day some years ago when he was talking to a group of schoolgirls. They had asked him about children (*criaturas*) their age, back in the time of Monte Verde, and he had shown them this boleadora, this plaything and the groove around the middle that had been carved with care, a dexterity that could only have been born of love. Somebody, he told them, some adult, had been fond enough of that child to spend long hours hewing that toy into shape.

"Look," he says to me, pointing to the *diapo* as he must have pointed at the object itself in front of the girls, repeating to me the words he must have said to them back then, "look at the ornamentation, how it was beautified, perhaps by the father, perhaps by the mother, the grandfather, perhaps for the child who left the footprint."

The schoolgirls had wanted to see the huella, and Mario had clicked the slide show until it reached the right diapo, projected onto the wall. *That foot,* he had said to his audience in the schoolroom, *was small, like this. Like one of you, a girl like one of you.* He had never before said anything like this, he tells me, and certainly never to a group of girls.

Mario had then felt, he says, the sudden presence of someone, a person, a small person, invisibly next to him. And out of nowhere, without knowing how or why, he had started to cry. The girls, after a stunned pause, joined in and then the teachers and soon they were all crying, all of them sobbing incontrollably. Mario had clicked off the slide machine.

And was haunted by the incident for days.

"I'm a nonbeliever," he tells me. "I don't believe in God. I don't believe in anyone but my friends."

Even so, the experience had been so strong and bizarre and palpable that he had approached an esoteric woman in Valdivia who was rumored to be in contact with spirits. She asked him to return in a few days' time and, when he came back, informed him that she had established a connection with the Monte Verde family that had lived those many thousands of years ago. One of the family was a girl, twelve years old.

Mario was skeptical. *Ask her a question,* he suggested, something that had not yet been published: Where was the opening of the toldo they had all lived under, what direction had it been facing? And the answer the woman had come up with was disappointing, absolutely wrong.

So Mario had discarded the idea that there were any spirits of those people hovering around. "But just in case," Mario adds as we head for the door, "I never used the same slide again."

We say good-bye in the drizzle of a typical Valdivia fog.

"When you describe them," he says, giving me a hug, "don't forget to describe them with songs at night, and nocturnal stories and … People imagine them all—growling and barking, like simians, hairy and very dirty—that's how we've pictured them. But a culture that knew so much about nature …"

On my three-hour trip back to the Puerto Montt airport, I realize that I have some time to spare before my plane flies off to Santiago, from where we'll start north by car, and I decide to take the thirty-kilometer detour to Monte Verde. If Angélica were with me, she'd scold me, warn me to watch out for the mud.

Not bad advice. I almost get mired down when I park my car just off the mucky road that borders the Monte Verde site. While I have been holding the huella in my clumsy hands and chatting with Mario Pino, here in Puerto Montt it has been raining persistently, the perfect way to masochistically prepare myself for the dry air of the desert I will soon be breathing.

But I do have one last question for Monte Verde. Why did they leave? Why did the men and women, why did the grandparents and the children of Monte Verde, suddenly abandon what had been their home? It had been sudden: They had left behind the utensils with which they had been working on a tree trunk just a few hours before their departure. Grain and food as well. And no signs of violence, no sense that the Monteverdinos dismantled anything in a hurry. They intended to come back and simply did not return. Did something happen to them, to the whole extended family, some disaster in some other place? To the child whose last act at Monte Verde may have been to leave that footprint?

The field of Monte Verde does not, of course, reply.

I venture into it one last time, now with no guide, no company. It is extremely wet and I semi-slip as I make my way toward the creek, leaving my own huella in the marshy mud—though I doubt that thousands of years hence someone will salivate at the prospect of understanding who trudged through here with his Asics jogging shoes. Maybe there is another footprint down there—overlooked by Tom Dillehay and company, who have only worked 80 percent of the site so future generations can explore what had been left unexcavated, with methods that might be able to shed more light on what happened here. Soon, also, other similar sites will be discovered and, researchers believe, a whole chain of Monte Verde culture will be revealed, all the way up to Canada. And then Monte Verde will not be so alone.

Meanwhile, a museum—called Monteverde, La Huella del Hombre, using the word huella not only as footprint but as trail, the wake of signals left behind by us in the land—will be built here, flanking the outer ridge of the original site, across from the dirt road I have twice used to get here. Tom and Mario and Eduardo are planning an ecologically integrated museum. In a gigantic central room, there will be a reconstruction of the site itself. One of its walls will be an entire window that looks out onto a forest and a large garden that should contain a mélange of plants, more than fifty with medicinal properties alongside twice that amount of specimens with nutritional value. It will take one hundred, perhaps one hundred and fifty years, for those samples to sprout: Visitors will be able to study them, walk down *senderos de interpretación* (interpretative paths) and even buy some seeds and take them home to their own gardens. An homage to the deep knowledge of the forest and fields of the Monteverdinos. The guardians of the museum will be the very Barrías who have taken care of the site all these years.

Mario Pino had told me that he sees Monte Verde as a challenge, a way of testing Chile. For a country whose identity in a world of accelerated globalization is under siege, questioned by homogenizing forces from abroad, here is an anchor in the past: ancestors who were centered in their own environment, who survived by depending on things they had created themselves. "We could learn," Mario had said, "from the way in which the Monteverdinos interacted with the forest, we could make the Earth ours in similar ways."

Such a possibility seems to me to be rather far off. Help for Monte Verde or its museum has not been forthcoming or exactly bountiful. Hardly any support from the university authorities or from the government or from the public at large. Dillehay is looking for outside funds.

The only consolation, perhaps, is that nobody will come to plunder this place. There are, after all, two ways to protect a site of such significance for all of humanity: One is to build a series of gates, hire security guards, surround it with alarms. The other way is through ignorance and neglect. Nobody can steal what they don't know is there. The best shield for Monte Verde may, paradoxically, be its utter lack of protection and pretentiousness.

I leave it there, that place with such spectacular implications for the history of the Americas, hiding its dramatic disruptions of accepted theories from any meddling eyes, much like it must have been before one of the Barrías chanced upon the tusk of the mastodon. If this sort of major archaeological find had been spotted in the United States, a quarter of a century later a dome would already have been erected to preserve the site, and hotels would have been erected in the vicinity, and tourists would be descending from large heated buses, cameras in one hand and candy bars (with wrappers) in the other.

I shudder.

Maybe it is better like this: just the cows, the geese, and the Barrías. And a bird that flies by every morning at the same time. And maybe, who knows, another footprint left by another child, down there, somewhere deep in the earth or under the quiet creek of Chinchihuapi, waiting to speak to us again.

If we know what questions to ask.

Star Prospectors

Saturday, May 11, 2002. Cerro Las Campanas.
One Hundred Miles North of La Serena.

We are standing on this hill at the top of the world, gazing up at the Magellanic Cloud of stars, staring straight through the clear midnight sky of the desert at the origins of the universe. Near to me, my friend Miguel points out constellations that may have died billions of years ago—and his wife, Jenny, and Angélica and myself, we nod and wonder and are somehow simply thankful to be here, the four of us quite simply sharing this moment of awe.

Five hundred kilometers or so north of Santiago, Angélica and I have taken a short detour off the highway, responding to a long-standing invitation from Miguel Roth, the director of this complex of observatories at Las Campanas, one of the most famous and powerful star-gazing facilities on the planet. An excellent way of starting our trip: to witness how the Chilean desert we are about to explore allows its visitors or inhabitants another sort of exploration, of time and space, a chance to probe how that time and space began, how the very minerals of the desert that lies ahead had their beginning in some cauldron of hydrogen billions of light years in the past.

Talk about origins!

These scientists and postdoctoral research students who are using the many telescopes on this hill to chart how galaxies change over the course of cosmic time are tackling questions that buzz in all human heads: How did we get here? What brought us to this point? And other, more specific, questions: Why are we standing on this planet that orbits this particular sun? Why is this star in this galaxy? How did the universe become the way it is?

One of the reasons why the answers have become more elusive is because here at Las Campanas, on February 24, 1987, Ian Shelton, a Canadian scientist using the very Magellan Telescope that gleams like a mammoth dome of metal right behind us, registered the explosion of a supernova. "It was up there in the Larger Magellanic Cloud," Miguel says, pointing to a batch of stars that seem to my naïve eyes imbued with a specially soft radiance, "and I wasn't here yet, Jenny and I had just returned to Chile from exile."

Supernovas are aging stars that do not want to die, but when they go, they do so spectacularly, with a bang. And the violent blast of stellar material recorded in 1987 was so close to Earth (only 163,000 light-years away) and released such an amount of energy (it was visible to the naked eye for several months before it began to collapse and decline) that it became the event of the century in astronomical terms. Because it allowed measurements and comparisons that had hitherto been unavailable to modern astronomers (the previous large supernova sighting had occurred in 1604), it meant a major leap forward in the theory of star evolution and the formation of the universe and how our own solar system was created. It also began to reveal some disquieting data: The universe that, according to previous theories and predictions, should have been contracting or slowing down or extending itself slowly into space, seemed instead to be *accelerating* while at the same time expanding—and there were, and still are, no explanations in quantum physics for how and why the universe created by the big bang fifteen billion years ago is acting in this entirely incomprehensible way. So that more or less at the time Roth came to Las Campanas in 1989 as a resident astronomer, he found the whole field of astrophysics in a state of whirlwind redefinition, desperately searching for a new paradigm with the sort of excitement that had not been seen since the start of the twentieth century, when Planck and Bohr and Einstein changed the way we look at energy and light and existence.

In a sense, everyone now working at the observatory is picking their way through the luminous debris left by that sensational 1987 supernova explosion, their lives and research dedicated to trying to track down one more breakthrough event that will confirm or deny the current theory of how the universe began and how it will end. While several of them—including two astronomers from Poland—look for something even more elusive: the dark matter that composes 70 percent of the universe and is somehow missing, as difficult to bring to our eyes as the forgotten past of our own human history.

Earlier in the evening, as the pink of the sky after sunset was turning into a darkening meadow of stars above, we had climbed up into the entrails of the Magellan Telescope, the command and control room where fifty screens and a zillion (or so it seemed) computers were buzzing and clicking and whirring data. Because there happened to be a mild cloth of clouds and unusually high winds, the technicians had closed down both this telescope and its twin, the Dupont Telescope, after only forty minutes' work. Just my luck—but the silver lining in this particular cloud was that the men (and the lone woman) doing the research had plenty of time to explain what they were up to. They showed me how a spectrograph works—the main instrument astronomers have for measuring the wavelengths radiating from the energy of a star, the redshift in the spectrum of starlight permitting them to figure out how far away, in time and space, a galactic system really is, and how fast it may be moving into the distance. I saw pictures of galaxies about five billion years in the past, captured in an amazing swirl of colors that would make any modern painter blue and green and red and yellow with envy, but that in their case—or at least in the case of Scott Trager, a postdoctoral fellow—helps to snare galaxies that are old and have ceased forming stars, in the hope of determining when that process stopped.

And still later, as the evening became deep night—yes, time passes on this Earth of ours as well, in infinitesimal increments compared with the cosmos, but ticking away nevertheless toward our own extinction—later, Jason Prochaska and Hsiao-Wen Chen, two young visiting scientists from Santa Cruz, showed me the spectrum of a quasar they had been studying, one that is farther away than any human mind can really grasp. How then are they able to deal with these outrageous time frames and overwhelming distances on a daily basis, and the answer was that they really didn't, they still had, in spite of the familiarity of it all—a galaxy after this meal, a comet for dessert, intergalactic gas with the cognac—incredible problems in imagining what fifteen billion years really meant. "This desert," Scott had told me, "is two hundred million years old and the Earth is four and a half billion years old and me ... I'm thirty."

Now, late at night, gazing up with Jenny and Miguel and Angélica at the wondering sky that the twenty or so astronomers cannot even glimpse from inside their closed chambers filled with measuring machines, the stars which are ours for a few free moments without needing to be translated into computerized graphics, ours whether we know or not that they are in reality godforsaken, faraway furnaces. I think of the scientists, all huddled in wait for the winds to hush and conditions to ameliorate so the night will not be lost, each hour at the telescope programmed one year in advance, parceled out as a reward for hundreds of pitiless twilights of wide-eyes, so valuable these hours at Las Campanas that not one of them will go to sleep until six in the morning anyway, just in case there is the slightest chance the technicians will relent and open the dome and let them, orphans of the cosmos, download the sky.

The next day before dawn—it is now Sunday, May 12—I awake early so I can witness the last stars fade from the horizon, and here come the astronomers, staggering and straggling into bedrooms where the thickest curtains and tightest shutters I have ever encountered anywhere keep the enemy sunlight from intruding on their daytime dreams. They are missing a stunning landscape as the first rays of our own Sunstar start to filter from behind the Andes and expose the many domes of the observatory, white and shiny and pleasing to the eye, strewn over several rolling interlocked hills, standing out against the rocks and bluffs saturated with reddish ocher shades. Like Martian vessels, I think to myself, that a genius set designer in a Hollywood flick has conceived, imposing some secret harmony, symmetry, geometric austerity on an indifferent hinterland. Not a speck of green or even of shrubbery taints the rigor of the meseta-valley, a broken vista of hues in ever shifting beige and tan so delicate that they manage to somehow soften the harshness of the parched land. Toward the west are more hills, part of the cordillera de la costa, shrouded at their base by a white cushion of smooth clouds, what the Pacific drifted in over the night and that will never rise to where I am standing.

I watch a bird suspended high above me, a condor or maybe an eagle, the sort that stays afloat for hours in the air, immobile, hardly moving or even gliding, just remaining there in one place with barely an adjustment of feathers, too far for me to perceive whether its head is turning slightly in search of a prey. I allow myself to hope—is the desert already exercising its callous influence on me?—that the creature will swoop down on something, a fox, a vizcacha, a dead guanaco, and give me a taste of the struggle for life and food that plays itself out relentlessly in backlands such as these. But the bird distances itself, disappearing upward into the wannest cirrus wisp that mists the sky and that may, if the prayers of the now-slumbering scientists are answered, dissipate by tonight. For now, Las Campanas is clean and clear, and over on another hill twenty miles across the canyon, another observatory, La Silla, run by a consortium of European countries, also twinkles away in the gleam of daybreak, its inhabitants also probably pleading for a translucent windless night. It is one of several other astronomical centers that have been built over the past forty years, scattered across the desert, the most recent one in Paranal, just outside Antofagasta, so powerful that its telescopes quadruple the range of Las Campanas.

The very same conditions that make the Chilean North so dry—high mountains in proximity to a coast cooled off by a chilly oceanic current—also create the special climatological circumstances that ensure that astronomers can happily settle in to capture the light streaming in from the heavens. I thought it was merely a matter of 365 almost cloudless nights a year, but just as crucial is the wind. Miguel Roth has explained to us—when we examined the Magellan Telescope itself with its thousands of mirror-eyes that devour and map out the light—what happens when the beam from a star hits the nocturnal atmosphere: Each ray is refracted and deviated by tiny invisible clusters of cells in the air, zigzagging from one to the other as it descends down to the telescope. If you can find a place where the winds do not cause turbulence, do not ruffle those cells, then you have what is called optimal image quality. And that is the case of this desert: The liminar winds that have already traveled thousands of imperturbable miles over the Pacific are constant and homogeneous on arrival, a stability that guarantees a smooth passage for the light coming from its source point billions of miles away. Which is why space telescopes like the Hubble are so valuable.

But certain spaces on Earth are also valuable, the North of Chile among them. This desert of ours does not only export minerals like copper, borax, iodine, lithium, and, yes, still some nitrate, but also the very sky itself, a sky of perpetual serenity, as it was described in the eighteenth century by the Abate Juan Ignacio de Molina from the exile in Italy into which the king of Spain had consigned him and all his other Jesuit brethren in Latin America: *la perpetua serenidad del cielo,* he had written.

Magnificent, no doubt, but day after day after day?

And this was only the Norte Chico, the small North as it is called, to differentiate it from the enormous expanses of Atacama and Tarapacá. Chico and small it might be, but nevertheless immense enough to start just outside the outskirts of Santiago. An endless series of arid hills had escorted us northward, hundreds of kilometers interrupted only by a sudden spurt of brush and sorry groves of trees barely hugging the hollow of a brook in the midst of sand and dust. And once in a while a valley and tunnels cutting through mountains and each hour one valley less and rocks, rocks, rocks on either side of the Carretera Panamericana snaking across the wasteland.

I was already a bit weary of it all, yearning for the rain of Monte Verde, the green mounts and cataracts of the Sur Chileno. And yet, there could be no better way to prepare for our incursion into the far more rancorous desert that awaited us to the north than this brief sojourn with Miguel and Jenny and the colony of astronomers. In one sense, of course, nothing could be farther than the ghost towns we will soon be roaming. Las Campanas is at the cutting edge of modernity, a marvel of imported technology—just as the *salitreras* once were in their own day. A tremendous infrastructure has sprouted up around these domes and these scientists in order to keep the cameras clicking and the computers humming and the hands jotting down dimensions. When Angélica and I first arrived at Las Campanas, we got lost among the maze of buildings—an electric generator, a mechanical support unit, housing for staff and workers, recreational facilities, a gym, a library, a minor medical center with an ambulance. Billiards, Ping-Pong, games of all sorts. Most of the astronomers and the technicians—and guests such as ourselves—sleep in the elegantly furnished rooms of the vacation-like mountain lodge where the architecture, the multicolored stones, the careful masonry of the walls, recall a small skiing resort in Colorado or in the French Alps. And like people on holiday, everybody here overeats, compensating for the desolation by wolfing down the tasty abundant food in a cafeteria-style restaurant. Cooked by a crew that takes turns going back to their wives and children in neighboring La Serena or Ovalle—because they, like everybody else at Las Campanas, do not consider this their primary residence. Two weeks here, two weeks down there. No matter how much aesthetic attention has been lavished on each detail to make it more tolerable for the permanent staff and also for the visitors who often spend months on end at these facilities, nobody calls these hills home. Nobody ever did, nobody ever will—except the occasional vulture and the many mountain goats whose droppings grace even the entrance to the world-famous Magellan Telescope. A contrast that was not lost on me, the dung at our feet as we scuffle to see the stars, those tiny stars of shit at the threshold of the lofty buildings that shelter the even loftier aspirations of reaching, touching, probing the mysteries of constellations billions of miles into the past. The animals that will inherit this place once it is—as it someday must be—abandoned.

All this hyper luxury, brought in from elsewhere. As in every desert, if the need to mine this particular resource (in this case, the stars from the sky rather than the minerals from under and inside the land) ceased to exist or could be better extracted somewhere else, this lovely, civilized, artificial enclave called Las Campanas would collapse.

The desert here, like the vaster desert that Angélica and I will begin to explore in the days to come, is a place where men cannot survive without that which they bring from the outside world. Beginning with water. I have only been traveling for two days or so and I already understand something about this hostile and cryptic terrain. You can immerse yourself in the sea or be welcomed by a forest, but the desert is incessantly reminding you of distances—between yourself and the rocks, between yourself and the next faraway human community, between yourself and your own endurance. The desert does not offer the illusion that you will ever be anything other than an intruder. Which is why I needed to drive through this region rather than hop over its majestic bleakness by air, as Angélica had initially suggested. No, I said, we need to have the experience of the grind of mile after mile. To feel the sand and the wind waiting to reclaim the space you have dared to build upon, the very road you travel. The desert: that mirage of eternity, or close to it, not really a void only because of the deep calm of the wild waiting patiently to wrap itself around you. Not like the woods where you have shade, protection, berries, leaves, brooks—where the Monte Verde people settled. They were trying to escape the desert, I think to myself, or their ancestors were if they first passed through these lands. Looking for a place where there was water, things to eat within reach of the hand, animals to be hunted down, someday domesticated.

Maybe they were running, without knowing it, from desert syndrome, a syndrome of loneliness caused by the desert—a psychological condition the reader will not find depicted in any manual of the mind because I have just coined the phrase, I came up with it, in fact, after a long conversation with Miguel Roth on this visit.

We have been friends with Miguel for over thirty years. Miguel and I, Angélica and Jenny had developed a deep comradeship and affection during the Allende presidency, those dizzy years of Chile's peaceful revolution, intensely sharing the joy and energy of liberation and later just as intensely living through the sorrows of defeat. It was not only the past that kept us in touch with one another during the arduous years of dictatorship and exile—meeting in Buenos Aires and in California and in Mexico City and in Amsterdam, wherever and whenever we could. Not only the memory of that time when life had seemed like a perpetual party, when we had all believed—we were so young and enthusiastic back then!—that we would emancipate our land, abolish poverty and injustice from the world; not only that joining us, not only the bonds that come from having faced death together and survived, but a fondness and intimacy that went beyond our common history, enhanced perhaps by the fact that Miguel had been born, as I had, in Argentina and had chosen Chile as his home and married, as I also had, a Chilean woman—the delightful Jenny. Not to mention that he is among the jolliest and smartest men I know.

I found Miguel as generous and gregarious as ever, wider in girth, his sandy-colored beard slightly graying, but the same bellowing laugh of yesteryear shaking his large frame from top to bottom. Intelligent and witty, quick in repartee, always ready for a pun or a game or a song, able to command in an easygoing, nonaggressive way, an excellent administrator and a first-rate scientist. Proud of what he's accomplished, glad that the Carnegie Institution, which runs Las Campanas, has entrusted him with directing such an important operation. But when we arrived at the observatory yesterday we also found him slightly on edge, easily irritated, as if not quite comfortable with himself or his surroundings—somewhat unexpected in the normally jovial Miguel. Jenny had offhandedly hinted when we met with other friends for dinner last year in Santiago that Miguel was starting to feel the toll of living far from her and far from home during 60 percent of each year. As our visit to Las Campanas proceeded, he seemed ever more relaxed, so when, in the course of our tour of the Magellan Telescope yesterday evening, we had come upon a leather couch in one of the wood-paneled offices at its base, I asked him to lie down on it and, pad in hand, acted out the role of psychiatrist, demanding that he confess what was ailing him. That's when I came up with the term—patented from now on—of desert syndrome.

Because it was the desert that had done this to him, eating away at the edges of his personality. Thirteen years of coming and going have impaired his ability to establish deep and significant human relationships, impossible with the transient population that ebbs and flows through Las Campanas but equally difficult to create with those friends in Santiago that he would like to hang out with on a daily basis—"and I just can't, I have to interrupt it all to come here, postpone those connections, unable to adjust here either, everything so fluctuating and artificial," all of this said in Spanish and then, suddenly, lapsing into English, "It's not a pretty life." And in Spanish again: "*Pero es lo que que hay.* It's what there is. This is what life dealt me." He was silent for a while again before he said: "I feel very alone here."

A typical dilemma, I told him, of those men (because most are male, in fact) who go off to work in places of intense isolation—on ships, in mines, on oil rigs, in wars—a dilemma that has to be fiercer in the desert, I would think. Even in the pampered conditions prevalent at Las Campanas, the landscape is there, imposing limits. "It's like a woman," Miguel had said. "It seduces, lures you in.... The first times you see it, the desert offers you many enticements and then it slowly denies them to you, it repeats the same offerings, each day almost despairingly rendering to you again what it already rendered yesterday. Always the same in its monotony. And you begin to realize that it will never really give itself up to you."

Nothing changes? I had asked.

Miguel recognized that, as time passes, he has been able to notice slight variations, be attentive to the ways in which the desert modifies its appearance. He sees guanacos from time to time, a burro, a buzzard. This year, for instance, there are a few more flowers, not as many insects, and a freak storm last September scared away the foxes that are supposed to eat the rats, and now the rats are gorging on seeds and grain and they love to eat cable—messing things up for stargazers and observatory technicians alike. Slim pickings of excitement for his urban and urbane personality.

And yet, as we burrow deeper into the predicament he finds himself in, this fractured life turns out to be a more perfect fit for him than he would initially admit. Miguel, the son of Jewish refugees who came to Buenos Aires from Austria after the Nazi takeover, has fallen prey to some of the same disintegrating forces that have pulled my own life apart. Like me, he fell in love with a country he had not been born into and been forced to leave against his will after the coup. And also like me, he spent the intervening years trying to return to Chile. But when he finally managed to come back, the country he found had been altered in some radical, almost sick, way. "When I returned to Chile," he told me, adjusting the couch so it would recline a bit more, "I had the sensation that I was walking along the street surrounded by people who had one of those paper bags over their heads, you know, with two slits for eyes. I couldn't recognize the faces, I couldn't recognize what people were saying, I couldn't recognize anything." The dictatorship, he felt, had changed people in deeper ways than the military had even planned. And yet this was now his country and the country of Jenny, this was where their two grown-up sons were settling down, there was nowhere else in the world where he might feel any less alien.

Times were tough in Chile in 1987 when they had made their return—Pinochet was still holding on to power and there was no place in a university system controlled by the dictatorship for a democratic dissident like Roth, and no job anywhere else for a scientist who had specialized in high-temperature physics (the topic of his doctoral dissertation at the University of San Diego). So when the Carnegie Foundation, impressed with Roth's years of experience at the National Observatory in Mexico, had offered him the post of resident astronomer at Las Campanas and very soon thereafter the directorship, he jumped at the opportunity. He has presided since then over some eventful years in the observatory's history, has supervised the complicated installation of telescopes on one of the hills where there had been nothing but crag and sand, and could be gratified at his success in running a major research center with efficiency and imagination. He might complain about the personal restrictions such a career choice imposed upon him, but this desert outpost allowed him to live in a way he would have desired anyway: to be in Chile and not in Chile at the same time, separate himself from the country he no longer recognized, his back-and-forth journeys in space a painful reminder of a similar mental journey of approximation and distancing he would have had to experience if he dwelled in Santiago on a permanent basis. He had gone to the desert out of need—but he had stayed there, I thought, for the reasons so many others have gone to other deserts and remained there years beyond their first arrival: because there was no better place for them in the world. The sort of existence Miguel would have had to live in a mainstream Chile twisted by years of fear, mistrust, and persecution would not have satisfied him either. It wasn't really the desert that had cracked open his life, divided it in two: It was the dictatorship.

And there was considerable comfort in his scientific research, the stars beckoning every night. Even if he had no formal training as an astronomer, even if he was forced to spend much of his time on administrative duties, he still has been able to plunge into the mysteries of stellar evolution.

We had talked about his interests last night, as we looked up into the depths of the desert sky with Angélica and Jenny. The enthusiasm and good humor of the old Miguel, the Miguel who is not fatalistic, poured out. How are stars born, how do they die? He is fascinated by the ways in which astronomy is linked to biological phenomena, inasmuch as both processes, our lives and the lives of stars, are not reversible. "There are certain moments that seem to hint at reversibility," Miguel said, "but they are somewhat like those intermediate periods in adolescence, when at times you're like a child, at times you're an adult. That back and forth, stars also do that, stars also resist entering, not death, as much as the geriatric stage of their existence.... Just like us ... " And along came that hearty laugh of his.

And because he loves graceful objects, he also has concentrated on the planetary nebulae, as aesthetically pleasing swirls of matter as you can encounter in the universe. What our sun will someday become. It will start to shed a large part of its material and keep a very hot core in its center and as it ionizes the material it cast out, it will look very beautiful as it dies.

"Even though," I said, "none of our species will be around to appreciate the spectacle."

Miguel shrugged. "Nobody there at the beginning either. The big bang must have been quite something to see, if there had been eyes to see, that is."

Origins. I had come here, to the North, in search of our origins and I was getting more than I had bargained for. By closing in on the beginnings of who and what we are, wasn't I running the risk of having to look as well at our ultimate extinction?

A sudden wave of existential terror swept over me, a terrifying solitude that is not a syndrome of deserts but of life itself, a dread that invades a human body when the lonely mind that commands it wanders to the edge of the edge of the cosmos, dares to try and imagine the distance corroding the desert of stars in the sky.

So what did I do? On that hill in the backlands of Chile where a supernova had first been sighted that overturned everything we knew about our stellar birth, I did what you should always do when you are lonely unto death: Seek some form of consolation from a friend. I did what you do when confronted by any desert: Try to tame the distance.

I asked Miguel if, after all, we weren't looking out at the far faraway cousins of the atoms that danced right here, in us, next to us, through us?

And Miguel told me once more, almost as if he were spelling out a fairy tale to a child, about how it had all started, how the atoms created in the first instants of the universe fifteen billion years ago had formed into molecular clouds and from there into stars and the stars into galaxies. He told me how the molecules up there are the same ones that produced the desert and you and me, he said, and Angélica and Jenny and this sky and the water that was missing from the desert and the minerals that had first been mined in this very region, silicon and carbon and gold and copper. He told me how everything on this Earth had been formed inside the thermonuclear machine of stars, the iron in the hemoglobin in our bodies that transports the oxygen through our tissue, the sodium and the potassium that became nitrate and fertilizer, our heart that beats and our brain that thinks and our memories themselves, all, all, all of it made from stars, formed inside a star.

"Somos polvo de estrella," Miguel said. To Jenny and Angélica and to me.

Some cause for solace, perhaps, in my quest for the origins. Miguel was telling me that we humans are, quite literally, stardust.

Cemeteries Under the Moon

Monday, May 13, 2002. Somewhere in the Desierto de Atacama.
I am standing in the middle of what used to be Oficina
Alemania, a nitrate town where thousands of workers toiled at
hammering *caliche* and pulverizing it and boiling it until it
released its treasure of white gold, I am standing where millions
of tons were lifted onto carts pulled by mules and then onto
trains and finally carried year after year over to the port of Taltal
so the fields of Europe could bloom with sugar beet and grains
and vegetables, I am standing in front of a small monolith with
the statue of a human figure on top representing the *pampino*
who harvested this desert as if it were a field of green and not a
crust of hard granite rock, I am standing in the middle—or is it
to the side?—of Oficina Alemania in the driest desert in the
world and I turn and look around and I see … nothing. Not

even the husk of an abandoned shack, not the hint of a silhouette of a ruin, not a photo op, nothing.

Just the horizon stretching into emptiness. And the garbage. Left by travelers who stop, gawk, unwrap their candy bar, take a bite, and hurry along on their way.

An ice-cream wrapper, a broken beer bottle, some crumpled toilet paper clinging to a piece of flint, that is what I see in Oficina Alemania. Even the name that persists, a misnomer. The first hubs of human activity erected to exploit nitrate, when they made their appearance in 1810, the year that most of Latin America proclaimed its independence, were originally called *oficinas de compra,* because they acquired *(compraban)* the slag brought in by independent workers. But they were transitory structures that hastily moved on as soon as the surrounding fields were exhausted, whereas Oficina Alemania, like so many similar nitrate towns, was a bustling permanent community with all the amenities of a small city.

Supposedly permanent.

Now less than a ghost town. Where are the streets first traced in 1905, the residences with their tin roofs of *calamina,* the company store sprawling over a whole block, the grand theater where the residents used to line up to watch Greta Garbo and Tallulah Bankhead and Pedro Armendáriz while a woman tinkled away on a piano to accompany the silent celluloid?

I remember Tom Dillehay's experiment in Monte Verde, his curanto picnic that had left no sign of its existence three years later. It has been over thirty years that this oficina—in fact, since it closed in 1970—has not had a soul sleeping or awakening here. What can possibly be left of the other nitrate production centers, hundreds of them, that ceased all activity many years before Alemania? How can not even the foundations of a building be left behind?

It all has been stolen. Even two of the four plaques on the monolith have been purloined, leaving only the statue itself—the life-size heroic figure of a man in bronze, one hand holding a sledgehammer and the other a flask, his two most loyal friends in the hostile desert, one to crack it open, the other to ward off its dryness. Beneath his feet, a maudlin inscription to those who worked and died here without thanks from anybody: *Pampino, thou wast the spine of this North and this country. Look thee now how desolate is thy land, far from that time of glory, from that flourishing land. Thy sons and daughters from this pampa remember thee.*

They seem to be the only ones.

"Look," Angélica says.

I am wrong. Something does remain. On the other side of the highway, a bit off the road, is a small cemetery. But I do not cross over to pay my respects to the people who used to walk by this very spot I stand on. For now, I'm anxious to touch for the first time the rocks from which nitrate is extracted, those pits blasted out of the desert seem to be beckoning to me.

I venture by myself into the surrounding expanse, trudging out as far as I dare, making believe I am lost. A silly game I like to play with myself whenever I visit an unfamiliar place: try to feel—pseudo-feel, might be a better word—the antagonism of an alien environment without really undergoing even the simulacrum of danger. I'd carried out this little experiment in locales as varied as the Casbah in Algiers (back in the seventies, way before it was genuinely perilous), the veldt in South

Africa, and the scrubland of thickets and bush called El Impenetrable in the northeast of Argentina. Mental acrobatics for tourists with a taste—but no more than a taste—for the exotic. Though what I am now trying to fathom happens to be my own history, my emotion giving to this wee incursion into the unknown a slight edge of urgency, even of intimacy.

So this is it, this is what it was all about, this is caliche. It is amazingly hard, this layer of rock that used to contain, several meters down into the earth, the salts and minerals that changed the destiny of my country and helped to feed the world. City pavement feels like tar compared with this. Just to push against this compact slab of stone with my fingers, to sense it adamantly resisting my feet, not bending to my weight or conceding an inch to my existence—is a lesson about the millions of hours, millions of muscles, millions of sweating arms that worked these salt flats to pry out the nuggets of nitrate.

Nobody knows for sure why this desert has so much *salitre,* as it is popularly called in Spanish. Theories abound, but they neutralize each other, kill each other off. Some say compounds filtered down from the mountains and then evaporated in the basin between the two cordilleras. Others suggest that the sea once covered this area and that a process of sublimation then produced this vast bed of salt and iodine. Still another theory proclaims that it was organic material, tiny microbes gnawing away over hundreds of thousands of years, that transformed the rocks into nitrate. Or hot springs.

No consensus.

Only one thing is certain, something on which all the experts agree: The lack of water, that curse upon this blighted land, is what blesses the desert with nitrate. All it would take is a couple of weeks of persistent rain for the salt to dissolve, for the salitre to disappear.

But it has not rained here for a million years and that is why, though nitrate can be found in many places around the world, California, India, Egypt, the Far East—and first used by Arab and Chinese and European alchemists (who called it "Greek fire")—it is only here, in the North of Chile, that the grade is high enough and the deposits vast enough to be exploited industrially.

I pick up a rock. If I had a match, I could try an experiment. In 1866, an expedition into this area in search of silver had been organized by José Santos Ossa. The grizzled miners, all of whom had learnt about prospecting in the thousand small mines of the Norte Chico that Angélica and I have just left behind, were camping for the night in the Salar del Carmen, not too far from this spot where I grip this bleached chunk of dirt and stone in my hand, and one of the team, Juan Zuleta, decided to douse the embers from his last cigarette using a small piece of pulverized white stone. When it began to sparkle and burn, he shouted "Caliche! Caliche!" All around, for miles and miles, were fields of nitrate like this one. And the salitre rush was on.

I don't smoke, so I won't be able to imitate Juan Zuleta. But this very rock that was split from the earth in a detonation some unknown miner set off who knows how many years ago can still fire my imagination. It was for this little piece of hard chalky earth that thousands of men left their homes, most of them seduced away from the verdant *sur* of Chile I myself was already missing, by the promises of fortune and a new start offered by the *enganchadores,* an escape from the bonds of the *latifundio,* a chance to be free. For this piece of earth they were packed into ships and came here with the hope of saving a bit of money and going back home and buying a plot of land and planting corn and potatoes. But they stayed, they stayed tied to this piece of nitrate compound as if it had been chained around their necks. They couldn't save a peso—they were paid in *fichas,* tokens that were only accepted at the company store of their respective oficina, where the managers laid down the law and enforced it with no outside interference. If the workers complained, they were whipped or could be fired, and if they lost their job, they had to leave, off into the desert, off to the next oficina, without more than the clothes they had brought with them, off to wrench another rock like this one from the land. This small aggregate of minerals making the hitherto despised desert the target of greed, a source of incessant prodigious wealth. So much so that South Americans killed one another in a war for the control of these resources, of this grain of salt: In 1879 Chile had launched what was known as the War of the Pacific against Peru and Bolivia, a war that ended with the victorious Chileans—who went so far as to occupy Lima—annexing these territories. Though that did not mean that the owners of this piece of rock I held in my hands were ultimately to be the Chilenos from the South, but rather a series of (primarily) British entrepreneurs and bankers who by the mid-eighties had managed to take possession of the majority of the nitrate refineries.

History must have a sick sense of humor, because the Englishman who would come to be known as the King of

Nitrate was called ... North, John Thomas North, and it was indeed that man from the North who owned, a few years after the war, the fifteen most productive *salitreras,* the four railroads that monopolized all transportation in the pampas, the Tarapacá waterworks that provided water to the whole region, and the businesses that imported European goods and distributed food to the oficinas. Many historians allege that North—who fraudulently bestowed upon himself at the height of his affluence the title of colonel—also engineered the successful revolt of the Chilean Congress against President Balmaceda in 1891, overthrowing the constitutional president because he was threatening to nationalize the foreign companies that controlled the production and export of most of the nitrate of the Norte Grande. What a twisted tale: the formidable Mr. North making sure that the wealth spilling out of stones like the one I now clutch in this Oficina would be used to keep similar stones in his hands and out of the hands of the people who presumably governed this presumably sovereign land. That thesis of an anti-imperialist Balmaceda—who committed suicide rather than surrender, eerily anticipating the tragedy of Allende eighty years later—has been disputed by other academics, but what no one doubts is how North's extravagant lifestyle epitomized the opulence of the speculators and financiers, mostly foreign and some Chilean, who became fabulously rich with the nitrate boom. Incredible to think what this tiny clod of earth could eventually build for North, how it would make him a pal of the Prince of Wales and a business partner of genocidal King Leopold of Belgium in rubber plantations in the Congo and let him lavishly entertain eight hundred guests at the Hotel Metropole in London in 1888, strutting with Lord Randolph Churchill and the Marquis of Stackpole and dressing up as Henry VIII while his daughter was bedecked as a Persian princess and his son as Richelieu, all of them waiting for a fanfare of clarions to call the company to dinner. That particular London bash—costing ten thousand pounds of the day—had been held to bid farewell to the Nitrate King on the eve of his new departure for Chile and was followed by many more parties he threw in Iquique and Santiago during the subsequent journey.

Festivities and feasts that did not last.

Here is the proof: this hole in the desert and the decay of the Oficina Alemania there in the distance.

Another war between brothers would destroy the fortunes made from nitrate and the towns built to replenish those fortunes and the lives of the men who had worked here. A European war this time, from 1914 to 1918, what was then called the Great War and is now known as the First World War. The desperate lack of Chilean nitrate and the interruption of shipments forced the Germans to find a substitute in their laboratories for what had been blasted from these domains of dust for the past forty or fifty years and had then been refined in oficina/towns like—well, Alemania, that Spanish name for Germany. I find myself in an ironically fitting place to recall how synthetic petroleum-based nitrate discovered precisely in the real Alemania turned the Chilean boom into a bust, that fertilizer much cheaper to produce in a chemical factory in Europe than to extract from a merciless desert on the other side of the planet. The fields of Flanders and the trenches of the

Somme devastating more than the lives of that generation in Europe; also shutting down the fields of the Atacama, closing the nitrate trenches of Oficina Alemania and Flor de Chile and Agua Santa and Bella Vista and Primitiva, and stranding in the port cities of Antofagasta and Iquique and Taltal and Pisagua and Cobija thousands upon thousands of discharged workers and their families who were no longer strangers to the pampa, who were by then *pampinos,* had forged a new identity in the *salitreras* and knew no other home.

Who had seen too many of their own die in places like these, too many of their children and spouses and parents and siblings and friends buried in places like these, to be able to ever really leave.

Do I have time to visit that cemetery on the other side of the Carretera Panamericana?

It is clear from Angélica's face upon my return that I do not. We want to reach Antofagasta, the largest city in the Norte Grande, before evening. We are having dinner with the novelist Hernán Rivera Letelier, who was raised in a town not very different from Oficina Alemania, and has written some searing texts about his experience. Better to speak with the living than to continue to torment the dead in demand of stories they will not be telling me. The *cementerio de* Oficina Alemania is not the last cemetery we will be seeing on this trip. And, in fact, it is not the first one we have seen today.

Early this morning, we had passed through the once prosperous port of Caldera, from whence had been shipped, in the mid-nineteenth century, the astounding silver of Chañarcillo, the third largest mine of its sort in the world at the time—as well as copper from a myriad of small quarries in the Norte Chico. Though now decaying, Caldera could still boast two noteworthy landmarks. One was a stunningly preserved railroad terminal, built by an American appropriately called Wheelwright, where on Christmas Day 1851 the first train in South America to carry both passengers and cargo had chugged in from Copiapó, a mining city snuggled in the mountains a hundred kilometers to the east—which also happened to be the first train in the Americas to ever reach the Pacific. The other major attraction of Caldera was the Cementerio Laico, the first non-Catholic burial site in Chile and probably one of the oldest in Latin America, established when Chile, before most other countries in the hemisphere, had separated Church from State. It was the railroad that spawned the cemetery: Many of its deceased residents are precisely the Protestant English, Scottish, U.S. citizens who had come to work on the railroad and the mines and had tarried on, MacKenzies and Griffiths and Smiths, from Swansea and Boston and Glasgow—though there were also a couple of pagoda-like mausoleums that housed Chinese immigrants and several Orthodox Slavs, all of them drawn by the wealth of the mining industry, like so many other foreigners would years later pour into the Norte Grande during the nitrate boom. A graveyard made more elegant and rueful by the exquisite wrought-iron fences that protected the tombs, crafted from the leftover materials of the train tracks and spare parts by the gringo artisans who were themselves resting right there, under our wandering feet. While our lips deciphered the faded epitaphs about God and love and forsaken homeland in twenty languages, perhaps readying ourselves for other burial grounds farther north where we would be trying to track down the names and lineage of Angélica's lost Iquique family.

But there was another cemetery that was awaiting me on the road today, the one place in the whole North I had passed through in 1962 when I had hastened onward to Peru and Bolivia that had left a lasting impression on me. With my two hitchhiking buddies we had been in the cabin of the enormous truck that had picked us up in the afternoon in La Serena—and the hours back then had passed pleasantly enough, with the driver talking to us incessantly about the sorrows of navigating these endless routes by himself, an early example of desert syndrome, if I had been experienced enough at the time to have noticed the symptoms and offer a diagnosis. At a certain point that night, the driver had stopped the truck some kilometers—twenty, maybe thirty?—past Caldera and suggested that we descend to relieve ourselves. But the real reason, he said as we clambered out, was different. *You* muchachos *will want to see this.*

And there it was, under the full moon, some forty years ago. What I would remember later, what I would try to describe to Angélica when I returned from that trip north, what had stayed with me through the years, had been a range of hollow rock formations stretching for a good kilometer, shaped by the wind into gigantic twisted skulls, phantasmagorically frozen in the moonlight. Something very ancient and strangely menacing in the white darkness.

I could not, of course, repeat the experience in 2002. This time there was no moon and it was gray and slightly drizzly—the same bad front of weather that had closed down the

Magellan Observatory two days ago on the Cerro Las Campanas chasing us farther north. And yet the intervening years had made the place even more ominous. Since I had last been here, my body had survived a coup, my mind had lived through exile and a dictatorship, my heart carried many Freddy Tabernas inside.

I braked the car and took Angélica by the hand and cautiously walked with her toward that scattered landscape of dark boulders. Almost exactly as I remembered them, strange and ghostly, carved from within as if they were screaming silently, one after the other, one after the other.

A cemetery of rocks, Angélica said quietly.

Why had they stuck in my mind all this time, those cavernous bodies of stone that forty years later still knew no rest? It may sound lyrical or overly intellectual, but I can't help but think that I was somehow back then anticipating the deaths of the future. Something at the threshold of that desert was speaking to me about incredible wracking pain and hollowness and time and loss and perhaps even, in some strange way, speaking also of resistance. Speaking so strongly that, in my memory, that place had always been the one essential portal to the North. And repeating forty years later the same inconsolable mourning of the rocks, forty years later telling Angélica and me what we would find, a desert full of ruins, a past that at its most glorious might have already suspected the future of ruination that lay ahead, all the dead oficinas knowing that it was just a matter of time before the desert returned to how it had always been, before paltry men had made tracks on its face and stolen its minerals and shipped them across the sea.

At the edge of the desert: the cemetery of rocks

I could safely skip the cemetery of Oficina Alemania. I had definitely had enough of bodies and bones for the day.

We climb into the car and head north.

"Next stop, Antofagasta," Angélica says, glad that we will not have to descend in darkness the cliffs that lead down to that port city by the sea.

I do not tell her that there is one more place I need to visit before Antofagasta, before the day is done. An antidote to the desert that I desperately need.

Not that I am put off by this drive. These last two days have been anything but monotonous. There are long hours, it is true, where nothing seems to change. But then suddenly there is a *cuesta,* a series of hills, like Portezuelo Blanco, and such a dizzying array of browns and grays and terra-cottas (Angélica's favorite color), all the hues that blend into each other and into something approaching whiteness farther on, and then a shining *arenal,* dunes of almost carrotlike pale red and then another granular slice of distance that wants to be the color of milk but can't quite manage it. And then there was a meseta made of darker clay, fingers and tongues of sand descending from it. And later a plain of such never-ending blue that it seems like the sea, seas of clay, seas of stone, seas of brownish blue, one of the few places in Chile so wide that you cannot see the Andes. Drunk with shades and pigments and tincture, so that I understand why so many come to the desert to get high on drugs and let themselves be gorged up through their eyes.

And then you are so very thankful when you see something as ordinary as a tiny tree, maybe it is a *tamarugo*—the species that used to cover parts of this desert and was used up to fuel the furnaces in the early days of the *salitreras;* and there is what seems to be a cactus, and farther on, that has to be a mirage in the desert, something like a city shimmering cloudlike on the horizon, no, no, it's—and then it disappears and your eyes focus on the road and what you're seeing can't be true either, but there is a man walking by himself on the other side of the road in the middle of nowhere, carrying a portable fridge on his side, the sort vendors have in stadiums at sports events and on the streets of the busiest intersections of cities, this man carting his ice cream around where nobody is there to buy and nobody to even stop and ask him what he's doing and I feel like buying something from him but we go on, we are consumed by the fever of the forward thrust of travel that often grips you when you are on limitless highways.

And *un arbolito,* Angélica exclaims excitedly—where the slightest surge of water appears and a tree next to it, that's where someone has built a house, the smallest of oases giving us some verdant hope. And close by, like a dog trailing a man, garbage, the refuse that follows our humanity around even in the desert. And side roads from time to time, inevitably lizarding off to a mine, abandoned or semi-functioning or about to be revived, the only reason why anybody would want to build a pathway in the middle of these shoals of dust.

And signs of the dead in the desert. *Animitas*—what you can find on every road in every corner of Chile but far more noticeable here because they stand out against the stark and barren background. Just about every six miles or so, a pile of stones, a cross, a sort of little chalklike sanctuary, in some cases even a miniature temple, to record where someone died violently and where it is presumed that the soul (the little soul, the animita) is still nearby, willing to intercede for the living with the gods or the Virgin or whoever commands the great beyond and can do favors for us. The small deaths and small dead that never made it into the cemeteries that begin to dot the horizon as we penetrate into the *salares* where nitrate towns sprang up. And then what seem to be mirrors lying flat for miles next to the highway, maybe satellite receivers and transmitters or devices to capture solar energy, so strangely, almost grotesquely, ultramodern in a desert where, if you deviate ten yards off the road, you'll find everything untouched and intact, exactly the way it was a million years ago.

Ways in which we try to mark the land as ours.

Messages in the desert. People who have come before us have stopped, picked up stones, reddish in color, and even redder contrasted with the wasted sand dunes behind them and used them to write their names by the side of the road—messages of love, short memories of hope and despair, dates, hearts. I feel a bizarre tenderness welling from inside me when we pass these words written on the skin of the desert, a melting away of the anger that graffiti in natural surroundings usually awakens in me, a comradeship with those people who touched the desert and left something, anything, embossed on its features, writing on the desert as if it were a page.

I was here, they are saying, *read me, I passed through....* Isn't that what I myself am here to do? Though I dream about penetrating its secrets, am I not just skimming the surface of this land in order to leave some sort of mark on it? Isn't this desert full of pictographs and petroglyphs and gigantic hieroglyphs left behind by its first inhabitants, the forerunners of the men and women at Monte Verde, didn't they also try to send a message we are still trying to decipher, writing in their way on the desert with the elements provided, stones as words and stones for ideas, by that same desert?

And that is why I prepare to stop now, as we approach the interchange where we need to turn off the Panamericana and take the highway west that descends toward the sea and Antofagasta, seventy kilometers away, even if it is already darkening, even if we are late and our novelist friend is awaiting our call.

Up ahead, to one side of the route, is a gigantic granite hand thrusting up from a slight mound in the desert. Yes, I did say a granite hand and I did say gigantic—towering twenty or so meters high—a smooth rock statue, this *Mano,* erected here in 1992 by the Chilean sculptor Mario Irrarrázaval as a way of commemorating the presence of humans on this land, both the Europeans who had arrived in 1492 and those who had made the journey so many millennia before Columbus.

Our answer to the desert, that hand.

What makes us human. That we cannot accept the void, the nothingness. That we all want to leave something behind, a huella, a trace, but not by accident in the mud, not just a chance slip of a foot on the way to somewhere else, but deliberately, at times even brutally claiming what we find as ours.

There has to be a reason why writing was born on the edge of the desert. Weren't the inhabitants of the great original civilizations that emerged in the river valleys only too aware of the dangerous wastes surrounding them? Wasn't writing invented as a way of seizing a piece of land—writing, in its beginnings, laying down the foundation of law but also establishing property rights, saying this piece of land is mine and not yours, and certainly not nature's, nature that writes its ownership of this Earth in ways different from men? Wasn't it fear of the emptiness that moved them? Fear of what the hollow rocks were telling us in those sands outside Caldera?

Trying to establish some form of permanence, that is what we do, this species.

On the road to Antofagasta: the hand in the desert

All of us, living in ghost towns though we do not know it.

With the illusion that what we leave behind will not be swept away by the wind, that something will remain against the corrosion of time.

Hand by hand, hand in hand.

Gloriously making believe we will outlast the desert.

SECOND PART: GHOSTS

Nomads of Nitrate

Wednesday, May 15, 2002. Antofagasta.
I ask the old man on the other side of the table the question one more time.

"Why didn't you want to leave?"

The old man, Eduardo Riquelme, is one of fifteen or so members of the Association of Hijos y Amigos (Sons and Friends) de Pedro de Valdivia, who are gathered here in this large conference room in the port of Antofagasta at the invitation of Jorge Molina, the *intendente* (governor) of this region, so they can tell me the story of their lives. Pedro de Valdivia is what joins them to each other—not that they are all remote descendants of the man who conquered Chile in 1540 but rather that his name was given to the nitrate town that these men and women lived in for much of their existence before it was shut down six years ago. It is my first chance to speak to a group of *pampinos,* and they have certainly confirmed much of what I had read in books and articles, seen in photos and films, about the suffering that accompanied the extraction and production of nitrate. None of those present at this meeting lived through the really dark years of exploitation before the workers wrested from the *patrones* and the government some elementary rights—the right to be paid in money, the right to be given severance pay, the right to strike, the right to publish their own newspapers, the right to vote in local elections, the right to compensation when an accident occurred—but they still have plenty of horror tales.

Their stories come at me so quickly, one picking up the narrative before the other has even finished, that I have trouble noting down their names, they don't heed me when I insist that they please identify themselves each time they speak. Gradually, nevertheless, a collective picture does emerge, and it is almost better and more symbolic to have this mosaic or chorale of voices struggling to bring back the past: an electrician called Héctor Torres, who remembers how precarious life was like before social security and a national health care system was adopted by the Popular Front in 1938, and Gladys Torrico, who saw three workers killed in front of her eyes during a strike, and Julio Gómez, who didn't want to believe that their town would ever be closed down, the words come tumbling out, one after the other, Elizabeth Villarroel, who tells me about the barracks where the unmarried men were shut up and curfewed as if they were animals, and another *pampino* informs me of a trip with his children back to see the Oficina San José, where he'd been born and found nothing there, and nothing in Constancia, where his mother had come into the world and Santa Rosa de Huara, all gone—*my house without a roof*, says another man, *the kitchen pillaged, even the cemetery had been looted.*

And Mario Bernal, who was born in a small house, no floorboards, not even gravel, just the bare earth—seven siblings sharing three beds on the ground with their mother and their *tayta*. *Not literature*, he says to me. *All this is true.* "The water was filthy.... You had to scrape away the mosquitoes with their long legs before you could drink from the water and the water full of scum anyway and we'd drop a piece of coal in it to clean it out. And the hard meat from the *pulperías,* the company store where we had to buy our food because my dad was paid partly with tokens only valid there. And you'd have to shit behind the *aromo* tree, no place else to do it. And the explosions."

"The explosions," a man named Miranda echoes, taking over from Bernal. "I was four years old. I remember that afternoon when my mother was boiling clothes to get rid of the bedbugs ..."

"Yes," adds another *pampino,* "on Sundays we'd take the mattresses out and kill the *bichos* with hot water."

"And then I heard," Miranda perseveres, "the sound of dynamite very close nearby, and someone popped their head through our door and said, '*Otro huevón que se mató,* another son of a bitch just got himself killed.' Not only accidents. A boy and a girl, they were just youngsters, less than twenty, and they blew themselves up, out of love they did it. Life was harsh."

Now it is Bernal's turn to interrupt. "True, but I can remember being happy there as a child. I can remember loving how the tea kettle boiled over from the coal stove. I can remember killing lizards, listening to the *patizorro* croaking as it flew over our heads. My tummy was always full—with potatoes, but I can't say I was really hungry.... Or maybe I didn't know better."

Miranda agrees. "It wasn't until I was ten years old and sent to Iquique and got my bottom wet with the sea, only then did I realize how we lived. Later I found out that my mother had baked extra bread every morning and gone out to sell it, had been sewing clothes, saving up so I could study."

Someone else chimes in: "When I was five or six, I went to my grandmother by the sea. It took eight hours to reach Antofagasta back then.... I was sent like a package—if my grandmother wanted me, she had to pay for my delivery."

"I became friends with Chato Valdés in Antofagasta," Miranda continues, unruffled, "who invited me to his house—there were floorboards made out of wood, I went to the bathroom and there was a toilet with a chain for flushing, I opened a faucet and water came out. And one afternoon I went to buy mortadella at the corner store and I saw a customer who said to the owner, no, not that one, I want slices from that one. I couldn't believe anyone could choose what they ate. In the *pulpería,* you bought what they gave you."

And yet my friend the novelist Hernán Rivera Letelier, who has been humbly sitting by my side while the *pampinos* pour out their stories, had also told me, just the night before, over dinner at the hotel where Angélica and I are staying, how the day the citizens of Pedro de Valdivia had been evicted, they had, all of them, cried. One of Chile's most successful writers in spite of having started life in the uttermost poverty, he had worked in that nitrate town for ten years before it closed down and had shared in the sorrow of the men and women in this room, the one constant in their lives—besides the inevitable sun rising like a demon each morning—the knowledge that this day would come, the certainty that some day they would have to move on. Hernán had watched town after town close down, at nine years of age the Algorta he had arrived at when he was less than a year old and then later Coya Sur and then Mantos Blancos and then Pedro de Valdivia. Families had packed their few belongings, they had climbed up on trucks, and, as they left behind the dusty streets where they had been exploited and that they would never see again, they had, almost invariably, these men hardened by sixteen-hour days of labor, these men who had buried more children than they had ever seen grow up, these tough miners who thrived in a culture that stigmatized any show of weakness as a sign of femininity and sissyhood, these assertive and calloused machos had started to weep like babies.

It was this second story, of homesickness, that slowly begins to filter into the previous story of abuse and endurance, and overtake it. Over and over, I was hearing that they had loved living in the desert, that they were desperately nostalgic, not only for the town itself, but for the way of life of the *salitreras*. Nor was it merely that this group I am talking with represents a special sort of *pampino*—the ones who escaped, the ones who did not die of silicosis at the age of forty, the ones who were not burnt forever by the scalding fire of the furnaces, the ones in this room who became, most of them, primary school teachers, educated men and women now in their sixties and seventies. Most *pampinos*, according to those talking to me here in Antofagasta, do not confuse the exploitation that they suffered when they worked in the *salitrera* with the *salitrera* itself, with the desert that they all profess to have an abiding love for, that they remember with fondness, particularly a childhood that, in spite of the hunger and the beatings, the discrimination and mistreatment, they recall as brimming with freedom and imagination.

And slowly—very slowly, somewhat in the way that the hoard of saltpeter is itself coaxed from the raw material of caliche, a long drawn-out process—I begin to extract from them the recognition that the Pedro de Valdivia they remember, one of the two nitrate towns still open during the last decades of the twentieth century, was a model community, with salaries above the national norm, free electricity, water, gas, first-rate cultural shows subsidized by the company, excellent sporting facilities, in fact, something akin to paradise.

I wish I were able to compare that idyllic vision of their hometown with my own experience of it. I had, in fact, set out yesterday, on Tuesday, May 14, on a trip to the one fully functioning nitrate town left in the world, María Elena, set out, indeed, with the most devout intention of passing through the nearby Pedro de Valdivia, owned by the same enterprise. I even had the exact address of the house where Hernán Rivera Letelier had banged out, almost clandestinely, his poems for ten years. He had explained what streets to stroll, which parts of the abandoned town to avoid. But I had never made it to Pedro de Valdivia.

Originally, I was to be accompanied on this part of the trip by Sergio Bitar, a friend of mine from exile who had been Allende's minister for mining and had therefore spent long months after the coup jailed on the freezing windswept island of Dawson off the bitter coast of Patagonia. Upon his return to Chile, he had been one of the leaders of the resistance against Pinochet, elected, when democracy returned to Chile, as a senator from the Norte Grande. During his eight years in the Senate (his second term had ended just a few months ago), one of his obsessions had become the preservation of the three old nitrate towns that remained, by a miracle, relatively unaltered many decades after they had been closed down. Bitar had been instrumental in creating with groups of *pampinos* a foundation that would administer the rescued *salitreras* as museums. So he had offered to meet me in Antofagasta for the three days we would be here and act as my guide. One of the activities he had asked the Intendente Molina to plan was this gathering of elderly *pampinos* and another was yesterday's ride to María Elena (and, if there was time, to Pedro de Valdivia, whose refineries are going full blast even if the town itself is deserted) so I could witness how nitrate is mined in all its phases. He would use the opportunity to talk with some executives of the company, Soquimich, that runs those operations, and see if he could persuade them to come on board philanthropically and help the foundation. But my friend Sergio had been forced, at the last moment, to fly instead to Washington, D.C., leaving me to carry out the schedule that had been prepared for him, which included a long stay at the guest house of María Elena.

And that is where I had been deposited yesterday a bit past noon by the chauffeur sent by Soquimich to drive me to María Elena—a town three hours north of Antofagasta that looked exactly like the photos I had seen of so many dusty tropical company towns erected all over the world, interminably repeating the Victorian model that the British Empire exported to every corner of the globe—the only nod to the American owners who had built it a dilapidated baseball field and a movie theater built by Metro-Goldwyn-Mayer. And the only patch of green in the midst of that desolation, the guest house where I was to have lunch.

Arriving at that building with its two majestic palm trees and large veranda and slatted windows, once the residence of the oficina's administrator and his family, was like stepping into the colonial past—all that was needed to complete the picture were ladies in long white dresses sipping juleps on the porch while dark-skinned natives fanned away the flies. It was a luxuriant bungalow-like mansion under the shade of magnificent pepper trees, nestled in a delightful garden, made all the more resplendent by its contrast with the surrounding encampment of monotonous low houses of flat corrugated tin roofs, the grubby woebegone streets wide enough for an army to march down. And even more familiar, what I encountered when I entered the building, what I had contemplated in countless films (think *Out of Africa*) or in South Africa itself. The spacious reception gallery was cool, bathed in soft light from above, the walls covered with art and mementos and, at its far end, a grand piano that may have amused a select audience fifty years ago. Branching out from this central vestibule were a series of

Salitrera *María Elena: the guest house*

impeccably furnished bedrooms where I was invited to freshen up and rest until lunch was served. An hour later a servant ushered me in to an elegant dining room with a mahogany table that could easily accommodate a good two dozen guests, but where only three of us were to sit while a white-liveried waiter provided successive waves of food.

Despite the hospitable welcome proffered by my host, Eduardo Arce, the manager of the *salitrera,* and his own guest, Dan Amit, an Israeli mining consultant, I was not entirely at ease. This lunch had originally been organized, after all, to entertain Sergio Bitar, one of the most powerful politicians in the country, a close friend of President Ricardo Lagos—and instead they were stuck with this notoriously contrarian leftist gadfly. But it was not only that: I feel uncomfortable whenever

I meet members of Chile's business class, all too aware of their complicity with Pinochet's dictatorship, which in the case of Soquimich was particularly egregious, as our dictator's then son-in-law, Julio Ponce, had been one of those who acquired these *salitreras* from the state when they were privatized in the early 1980s in what observers consider dubious circumstances. And Eduardo Arce hints, at some point between the abalone and the sea bass—or was it just before we were served the meringue dessert?—when I inquire about his family, that his father had been traumatized by the experience of losing his hacienda in the South during the agrarian land reform program of President Eduardo Frei Montalva in the late sixties—a process carried out by some of my best friends. But this is also Chile—a country where people, at least of the elite, sit in close proximity to their former enemies and smile and chat about vintage wines and make believe the past does not really exist, that Arce is not a supporter of Pinochet and that I have not come to the North to search for the disappeared body of Freddy Taberna, not mention that Arce would lunch tomorrow at this table at the same time when I would be seated at a table in Antofagasta with the *pampinos* who were evicted from their homes because of decisions taken in the very room where we were having our midday meal. We talked instead about María Elena and its future—and on this subject I was visibly impressed both by the efficiency of the company and its ambitious expansion plans. As I would be later in the afternoon when Jorge Araya, the resident head of engineering, took me on an extended tour of the industrial complex.

Nitrate is invariably found intermixed with other minerals and the process of its production consists, back when it was first mined in the 1500s as well as in the twenty-first century, of grinding into smaller pieces the incredibly hard crust in which it is embedded, and then leaching those lumps of stone in water until the salt has been isolated and turned into crystals. What has changed over the centuries has been the technology employed to carry out this operation. In the early nineteenth century, small-time miners used mallets to wrench from the earth clumps of raw nitrate and then carried it, on mule or on their own backs, to oficinas where the slag was dissolved in boiling water and further refined in large vats under the sun, a rudimentary method of lixiviation that only worked with high-yield grades of 60 percent or more. That these oficinas were called *paradas*—meaning a place that you stop at, that is here today and gone tomorrow—indicates how precarious and transitory these encampments must have been, incessantly moving from one exhausted field to the next one.

It was only in the mid-1850s, when Europe began to demand more fertilizer and a Chilean, Pedro Gamboni, discovered a way to purify lesser grades of caliche at a lower cost, that the oficinas became stable settlements. Two decades later, Santiago Humberstone, a young British chemical engineer who had studied the Shanks system of refining caustic soda invented in Lancashire, applied the same method (steam pipes to warm the cauldrons) to caliche, allowing nitrate to be extracted from raw material that only had a 13 percent grade. The Shanks system allowed Chile to supply, by 1910, 65 percent of the world's nitrogen-based fertilizers. Twenty years later, when the German synthetic product had triumphed, the Norte Grande satisfied merely 10 percent of the planet's needs. If the depression of the 1930s that dealt a death blow to most *salitreras* did not, however, mean the absolute end of the nitrate cycle, it was because in the previous decade a new technique that further cheapened the extraction of natural nitrate had been discovered. Known as the Guggenheim method because it was adopted by Elias Cappelans Smith from methods prevalent at the Guggenheim-owned copper mine of Chuquicamata, it allowed the profitable opening of two new oficinas, María Elena in 1926 and Pedro de Valdivia in 1931—the last ones ever to be inaugurated.

What I had seen in María Elena (named for María Elena Condon, Cappelans's wife) was not, therefore, what I would have seen if, many decades ago, I had visited Oficina Alemania (or any of the more than three hundred other oficinas that once used the Shanks system and have all been abandoned), but it was at least, no matter how modernized present-day operations may be, a decent approximation of what it must have been like.

Our four-wheel drive Jeep started by driving past several heavily guarded security gates through a labyrinth of dirt roads so many kilometers out into the pampa that the only signs of María Elena on the horizon were the gigantic chimneys spouting smoke into the transparent air of the Atacama desert. We finally arrived at a *cantera,* the bottom of a quarry a hundred meters long by about twenty-five wide, where dynamite had been discharged that morning. I stood under a towering wall of caliche, four to five meters high, a veritable canyon of it, watching gargantuan excavators remove the raw material and lift it onto even larger trucks. If I wanted to see how the geologists decided where to blast—they break open the caliche and measure the grade of the ore by how it sparkles!—and witness the sticks of dynamite encased in their yellow plastic being exploded every fifteen meters, the thunderous sounds, the dust smoking up from the desert, Jorge Araya suggested that I could stay the night and watch it early next morning. I was tempted to accept his invitation—the rebellious history of this region is entangled with the history of explosives. It was, for instance, the dynamite in the hands of the workers that had led to an extraordinary anarchist insurrection by large contingents of Chilean and foreign workers in 1925. They occupied dozens of *salitreras* in demand of better wages and democratic rights, and victoriously fought off for many days the most powerful army in Latin America, though it had all ended with a massacre—do revolts ever end otherwise in my sad continent?—of thousands of insurgents in the oficinas of La Coruña and Maroussia. So yes, I was more than fascinated by any chance to witness the violence of the desert—even in the restricted scientific way it might be unleashed on these craters. But I had to get back to Angélica tonight and the *pampinos* awaited me tomorrow morning, so I would have to forgo that most spectacular of mining experiences, the moment when the desert is broken open and wounded. This image of a wounded desert deepened in me as we followed the trucks to a ramp where the mineral was deposited and crept upward to be crushed two times over, by what are called the *chancadora primaria y secundaria*. For miles and miles around María Elena—and every other salitre field Angélica and I had seen as we passed through by car—the earth

Salitrera *María Elena*

looks as if it had been shelled and shocked. Pockmarked, assaulted, hollowed out.

What this means, from the productive point of view, is that, as the deposits are depleted, the company needs to fan ever farther out in search of new beds of nitrate. Araya took me to the conveyor belt that carries the lumps of mineral—now reduced to ninety-ton blocks—and we followed its flow over fourteen kilometers as it carried the precious cargo to the refining plant where the Guggenheim method of lixiviation kicks in—after, that is, another round of mills grinding away at the stones. Speeding along next to the endless conveyor belt I could understand why Eduardo Arce had told me at lunch that a day might come when Soquimich would have to abandon María Elena and establish an entirely new industrial complex in some unblemished outer reach of the Atacama. The move was not imminent—at least that is what Arce assured me when I mentioned rumors about a possible closing of María Elena—given that they had nitrate in the immediate vicinity to last them for thirty, maybe even fifty years. But the farther they have to travel from the center to pry out the nitrate, the more expensive it will become, and at some point the cost of transportation will make it prohibitive to keep María Elena open.

To see this industrial process in its many bustling phases and accompany it patiently through all the different steaming and leaching and evaporating vats—updated with the latest technology inside the buildings, but outwardly the same structures built in the twenties and thirties—gave me some sense of what it must have been like over a hundred years ago when the voyager came upon these immense webs of human activity after crossing wastelands where not even a reptile crawled. And then to finally approach the blazing hills of milk-white crystals, to finally touch the nitrate and smell and taste it, again helped me to imagine life in the *salitreras,* how life poured into this desert and how it was pressed out. Though this is not the same nitrate of yesteryear, in fact. To survive in the global marketplace, Soquimich has had to tailor its production to the demands of clients from Japan to France to the United States and a hundred other countries, agribusiness that needs a natural fertilizer so soluble and easily absorbed that it can furnish a better yield to crops than synthetic materials. But what really separates this operation from what used to happen in the past is the emphasis on generating what used to be the subproducts of nitrate that now constitute the main sources of revenue. And when I asked Jorge Araya how essential those other minerals could possibly be, he pointed at the tools of my trade, iodine for the photos I was taking, lithium for the rechargeable batteries of my videocamera and recording machine, and borax for the eyeglasses I was wearing and the dental cream I had used that morning to wash my teeth and the detergent with which my clothes would be cleaned. I thought about that: the Chilean desert scattered almost invisibly to every corner of the globe, stirring inside a snapshot taken in Sri Lanka and a tomato eaten in Chicago and a toy truck running on batteries in Tokyo.

"Time to go back," Jorge Araya said. "I'm sorry you won't have time to see Pedro de Valdivia, but it's a long detour and your wife will be worried if you arrive too late. Never keep a woman waiting too long."

I liked Jorge Araya. A former army officer who took pains, without my prompting, to distance himself from the "excesses" of the dictatorship, I think I would have liked him anyway, with his mustache and bristling energy and willingness to answer every question frankly, how he reacted when our tour was interrupted because of a reported accident. He listened carefully to my theory about desert syndrome, but did not feel that he fit into the psychological model I was fantasizing about. Like most of management and an increasing number of workers at María Elena, he spent half his week here and commuted to Antofagasta the rest of the time—the sort of shift that I had already encountered at Las Campanas—but he does not consider himself at all lonely, perhaps because his military training prepared him for long days and nights alone. "This is what pioneers do," he said. "No desert is conquered without people like me."

But this is not what I remember now, the next day, this Wednesday, May 15, as I speak to the *pampinos* in Antofagasta. It is not the hint of that bond established between myself and Araya, the sort that men develop when they go on field trips together, that is not what comes to my mind. No, what I remember is something Araya said as our tour was ending, as we wound our way back through the sad streets of María Elena when I had asked him how he got along with the local authorities.

"*A las mil maravillas,*" he responded. "They have to get along well with me. I'm the real mayor here, not the one who is elected by the voters. If he wants to do anything here, like bring a circus into town, do or undo something, anything, he has to ask me for permission. I'm the one who decides. Because the whole town, every inch of it, belongs to Soquimich."

So this mild-mannered man with whom I had spent the most pleasant of afternoons would be in charge of evicting the inhabitants of María Elena if that town were ever to suffer the fate of Pedro de Valdivia. And this is the flip side of all the benefits, all the free electricity, the great sporting facilities, the inexpensive cultural events, the low-rent housing. The company that is responsible for garbage collection and street repairs and fixing a traffic light that has broken down is the very one that can extract the residents from their dwelling places as if they were pieces of mineral.

It is what Soquimich did with all the men and women gathered around this table at the Intendencia in Antofagasta.

It is what it did, above all, to Eduardo Riquelme, the director of the school at Pedro de Valdivia, the eighty-year-old man who, according to everyone else in the room, was the last person to leave that town, who stayed on even after the authorities had turned off the electricity in what had been his house to force him and his wife to depart. *"Riquelme fue,"* his companions insist, *"el que apagó las luces,* the one who turned the lights off." Which is why I have zeroed in on him, asked him why he did not want to leave, what had kept him there till the very end, six months after the last of the other Pedrinos had said good-bye?

Riquelme had not even been born in Pedro de Valdivia. He had arrived in that town in 1952, a thirty-year-old primary school teacher who was looking for a place in the desert where he would not suffer asthma attacks. The night he had descended from the train after an arduous three-day trip from the south, it was so late that he could not find lodgings and had made his way to the local police station where, after announcing that his father was a police sergeant, he had been afforded a cot for the night. The next day he awoke at dawn, shaved, and set off to report to the school. A few steps and he slipped in the dust—*"me di un costalazo,"* Riquelme says, laughing, "I fell down." Instead of seeing that as a bad omen, he thought to himself, *"Ya pagué el terreno,* I'm already paying for the land. That's how, I thought to myself, this earth is telling me to stay, that I shouldn't ever be separated from her. And I stayed on for forty-four years."

He says all this in a rich, mellow baritone voice that is all the more surprising because he is a small man, physically small at least, with precise gestures and premeditated pronunciations, a man used to giving public speeches and making himself clearly understood.

What was it that he liked so much about that *salitrera* town?

He mentions, of course, all the benefits—they all do, the Pedrinos—but he goes on to detail other traits of that community, which, once again, connects me back to what it must have been like in the heroic days of the pampa when men started arriving from other places, what they found besides exploitation and a hard sun under a treeless sky.

Pedro de Valdivia was a magnet, he says. He loved it that people from all over Chile came there, everyone with a different story to tell and a different lineage to defend. "Conditions in the desert are so harsh and life is not easy," he says. "You need the person next door more than if you were in a big city. You have nothing but each other in order to survive. So solidarity among us is stronger, more necessary than anywhere else. And that leads to a culture of tolerance and participation." He pauses. "I thought my wife and I would remain there until the pampa ended or until my life ended. Instead, it was the town that ended."

"Though we didn't want to believe it," one of the *pampinos* interposes, it may have been Angel Lattus. "I was born in Oficina Vergara, but Pedro de Valdivia was my home."

I turn back to Eduardo Riquelme. His emotion is real, his pain is real, and yet I don't feel that he has convinced me of how and why he was attached to that place. His explanation sounds a bit abstract, schoolmasterly, as if he were reciting a text. I want to press him a bit more. Pedro de Valdivia had closed in January 1996 and he had remained until June of that year. I ask him about those six months when he and his wife had been the sole inhabitants of what was now a ghost town, I ask him about the last night they had spent in their home before they had been forced to leave.

"Look," he says, and though I think he is changing the subject, he is in fact going to answer me, "I'd arrived at that house in 1964. And almost immediately, I started a garden.... There was a sort of an almost dry tree trunk that wouldn't come out, no matter how much I dug and pulled and tried to root it out, the tree wouldn't budge. It still had some branches growing. Not very thick—about like a broomstick, but it resisted. So I started to water it. And in 1996, when we had to leave, well, it was still there and I couldn't take it with me. So we stayed on. At first they just let us be. Then they cut off the electricity.

"Still we stayed on, cooking on a little stove with coal. But then they said they were going to turn off the running water. In June, that was 1996. So there was nothing more we could do. Well, we'll just have to leave. So that day we spent it putting all the plants in baskets. And that night we prepared the last meal in our house, where our children had been born, we talked about how life had been so good to us in that place. And before going to sleep, I watered the tree for the very last time, *por última vez*. In the morning I made us some coffee in the *brasero*.... The kettle was so blackened from the coal stove that we just left it there. We'd never be able to clean it up. For thirty-two years the bed had been facing east/west.... And just before we left, we placed it in the north/south direction. Because we didn't want it to remain the way it had been all these years. Our life was starting over. And the bed shouldn't have to keep any bad memories when we left it."

And he never went back to see it again, the house, the tree?

"We are born," he says, modulating that voice that reminds me of men who sing in barbershop quartets, in a choir, in amateur opera contests, "and as soon as we are born we start to die; each one of our experiences dies instantly and what keeps us going is the remembrance of those joyful moments. But we should not try to repeat them."

There is a moment of silence.

I ask him what he does now, what they all do.

They have a center in Antofagasta, a sort of social club, but Riquelme and some of the others have also created something they call Hermandad de la Pampa, a Brotherhood of the Desert. They spend many days visiting old abandoned towns, from Taltal to Pisagua, along eight hundred kilometers of desertland. On November 1, the Day of the Dead, Riquelme says, he makes a point of visiting a town he has not gone to before. He brings flowers and fixes up one tomb of an adult and one of a child. He doesn't know who they are, he just chooses any two graves. "These are the people who made Chile rich," he says. "And there is no memory of them. The martyrs who were massacred, who died, who built this country. I go to those abandoned oficinas to atone for the sin of amnesia committed against those dead."

I think about Oficina Alemania and the cemetery I did not have the time to see. I ask him to describe the last *salitrera* he visited.

"The last one?"

Well, any *salitrera* he wants to tell me about.

"Cecilia," Eduardo Riquelme says. "Cecilia was the most

modern of all the *salitreras*. Based on plans brought from San Francisco, California. I play the accordion and I decided that I wanted to play in the theater of Cecilia, the ruins of that theater there in Cecilia, and that's where I spent my day. I can't see Pedro de Valdivia despoiled, with the dust settling more every day, the wood being stolen day after day, but those ruins of Cecilia, that's different."

Our own ruins hurt more, I say.

Riquelme nods his head.

"So that day," he says, "there I was at Oficina Cecilia, near Chacabuco, and I took a folding chair, set it up in the theater, because I wanted to be there by myself.... I've spent so much time with people all my life that I needed a space for my solitude.... And I spent the whole day with a tin of tuna, *un limoncito,* a sprinkle of lemon, a bottle of *cerveza,* and I started to play the accordion, all by myself. I play for myself."

And now Eduardo Riquelme pauses.

"For myself," he says. "And for the ghosts."

Time for a Story

Thursday, May 16, 2002. Leaving Antofagasta.

We are standing in the midst of the ruins of Pampa Unión, a town that did not produce even one ounce of nitrate, a town that produced instead pleasure and indulgence and illusions, a town of brothels and bars, opium dens and gambling joints, a town only visited now by the whirlwinds and the shifting sands.

I know about this town—and we have stopped here, two hours east of Antofagasta on our way toward the mountains—because its story was told to me last night by Hernán Riviera Letelier. In *Fatamorgana* (one of the few novels by him I had not yet read), he sets his characters in Pampa Unión, a town that sprouted in the desert in 1912 to serve (and service) the twenty-seven surrounding nitrate communities, only to disappear forty years later, like a fata morgana, a mirage devoured by the desert. A mere twenty residences of Pampa Unión officially strutted the title of whorehouse, but in fact there were over two hundred of them: In every boardinghouse, in every grocery store, in every liquor shop, in every warehouse, the ladies of the night presided. The town became so corrupt that at one point the authorities had to dismiss the whole police force. But none of the policemen left. They stayed on in Pampa Unión and the next day there you could find them, each former officer of the law, administering a brothel.

I wander among the crumbling walls of this place of perdition. Pampa Unión has fallen into ruin the same way in which it was built—chaotically, with no apparent order. No systematically laid-out streets on the British colonial model here, no rows of obedient small houses, no company store, no central square, no sporting facilities built by the authorities, no trade union headquarters—and no church, because the Bishop of Antofagasta refused to erect a temple here, implying that those souls were too lost even to warrant a priest. Or maybe scared what would happen to any minor emissary of Christ in that den of vice, the only spot in the whole desert where there were more women residents than men, where those who worked did so at night and not in the blazing sunlight, where what was being mined was something else (in fact, loose women were called *minas*). A place of lawlessness, like the frontier towns in the Wild West of America that fascinated me as a child in New York, where the discipline and prescriptions of power that reigned elsewhere in the merciless pampa could be momentarily suspended, where sin was rewarded and passion could spill out.

I stand inside what must have been a large reception hall, maybe a saloon. Almost square in its middle, the twisted stump of a tree blooms, germinating from who knows what hidden well of water, what hidden memory of past voluptuousness. I kick through the debris toward the back, where a series of bricks and stucco delineate the cubbyhole rooms where love was dispensed by the hour to desperate men. Hernán Rivera Letelier's pithy statement comes back to me: "Where there is a miner, there is a prostitute—of that you can always be certain." I warily step over the scraps of what must have been a protecting wall, straight into the sun again. I wonder where they held the cockfights, how the liquor was delivered, who escorted the drunks out at dawn, what sort of post-coital card games were still being played as the sun came up.

Now a train is approaching in the nearby distance. I had taken a train just like that one in 1962, returning from my trip to Bolivia, I had followed this very route, passed by Pampa Unión all those years ago and had not even realized it existed.

No station then in Pampa Unión and no station now, but there was a building where trains stopped back then in 1929, the year when Hernán's novel takes place, the day that the dictator of Chile, Gen. Carlos Ibáñez del Campo, who had been touring the North, was going to pass by this town on his way back from Calama, solemnly installed in a special wagon that the English-owned railroad offered him. The train had to halt in Pampa Unión to fill up with water. The townsfolk organized a tumultuous reception for the president. Everybody poured into the station, all the harlots and the pimps and the barmen and the cardsharps and the miners from every nearby *salitrera,* and their families and the children. All of them feeling innocent and spry that morning when they awoke with the promise of some sort of regeneration before the day was to be over.

Hernán had described the scene to me and Angélica in his house on a hill high above Antofagasta, he had spoken about the flags that were waved, the tension mounting, and now, the next day here in Pampa Unión, I can almost behold it in front of my eyes. The band of musicians is ready, they've been practicing for weeks. The children are waiting to sing. The train is coming, the train can be seen chugging on the horizon. And people begin to cheer and they are hushed by one of the organizers. Things have to look orderly and nice. They want to use the occasion to ask the president if he could bestow upon the town some sort of legal status, recognize them as a municipality, put them on the map.

Accept them into the fold of the great Chilean family.

"And the locomotive," Hernán had said, taking his time, savoring our interest, "pulls into the station at exactly 3:08 in the hot, transparent afternoon."

En la tarde calurosa y transparente.

But the tale was interrupted, at that precise moment, by Hernán's wife, Mari, who came to tell us that the *onces-comida* was served. An evening meal that is an institution in Chile that combines a sort of English high tea with a Spanish dinner, that name *onces* presumably coming from some monks who would, the legend goes, repair in the long thirsty afternoons to a stash of *aguardiente,* referred to by its *once* letters, the eleven letters in that Spanish name for brandy, for firewater. Mari had a different kind of feast for us. She had prepared *pastel de choclo,* the most typical, mouthwatering Chilean dish, something like a shepherd's pie made of corn—and had done so because she remembered that I had published many years ago a book of poems with that title. A hospitality and attentiveness that made me understand why Hernán kept on saying that Mari was the best thing that had ever happened to him made me linger on the scene of their first meeting many years ago in Mantos Blancos, where he had gone in search of a job.

"I met her," he had told Angélica and me, "the way most couples meet in the pampa, in this part of the world. An unmarried man would arrive at a *campamento*—and 90 percent of those who came to work in the salitre fields were originally bachelors—and he'd ask, just like I did, so which house serves good meals and next day there you'd show up, trying to be on your best behavior because there were always two, three daughters who brought the food to the tables. Mari was sixteen and I was twenty-two. And a few days later I realize that in my plate of *cazuela* the piece of chicken was always bigger than anybody else's, and so was the potato." Many years later, it would be Mari's cooking that would allow him to write his first novel—paying with baked goods and meat pies sold house to house for the computer upon which he banged it out. A situation that repeats itself across the world whenever and wherever life is hard, but that seems especially typical of the *pampa,* that I encounter every time I hear a story from the *salitreras:* the mother, the wife, the sister, the daughter, slaving overtime so that her man can escape the inferno and, who knows, at times even take her with him as he departs.

Not that the two of them were thinking of escape when they married and went off to Pedro de Valdivia and Hernán had been sent off to the nitrate fields—considered the hardest sort of labor, almost like a form of punishment. Turned into a blessing, because that's where he had heard all the stories of the pampas that flowed out of the other workers as they made their way to the pits on trucks or afterward while they all rested. He would listen, he had told us, to the *viejos* for hours. Called viejos, old men, not because they were that elderly—miners tend to die young—but because they looked old and they took their time speaking and they were brimming with enough memories to fill several lifetimes. Memories and stories that Hernán coaxed out of them and that would later make him into a best-selling author, one of the very few writers in Chile who can make a living writing books. An extraordinary attainment for anybody, but more so for someone whose mother died when he was nine and who had found himself selling newspapers on the streets of Antofagasta to feed himself after his father had been forced to look for work in the desert. Even stranger, perhaps, his success as a novelist when we hear that he was the most timid child and adolescent imaginable, *silencioso, solitario y soñador,* a dreamer, solitary and silent, as he describes himself in *Himno del Angel,* his most autobiographical novel.

A listener. One of his first memories was eavesdropping on adult conversations in Algorta—"we lived in the poorest house on the poorest of three really poor streets"—where his mother and sisters, just like Mari and her mother many years later, helped to pad the family budget by offering meals. So that every night forty or so viejos would make their way to the

Rivera household for some tasty hot food and little Hernán would spend the night under the table, hearkening to their every anecdote. Fascinated by that capacity to weave words that he did not seem to possess, mesmerized by the sermons that illiterate evangelicals (his own parents were born-again Christians) delivered on the street corners of Algorta, totally bewitched later by the *charlatanes* in the alleys of Antofagasta, quacks and swindlers and peddlers who would beguile people with their masterful palaces of language, all those *ángeles del verbo,* those angels of the word accumulating inside him, inside him, inside him, *dentro, dentro, dentro,* Hernán said, until it finally began to come out, for many years as poems and then, one day in 1990, in the form of a story that grew and transmogrified into a novel, set in a whorehouse in the pampa and haunted by the lost world of the *salitreras,* the desert that was his first love.

And his earliest memory.

"I was sitting in a little straw chair—maybe I was three years old—and there was a tin door that opened up onto the pampa, right next to the kitchen made out of bricks and mud and there it was, the desert, it just swept into my eyes and invited me to come to it, that was my patio, that was my playground." And he had accepted that invitation. His favorite game: to catch a whirlwind, to jump in its middle because the legend said that if you opened your eyes in the very center of a whirlwind you could see the face of the devil, but of course the only drama that befell the kids was sand in their eyes. And his other early memory: trains that kept passing and passing, day and night. That landscape defining the hidden themes of his future novels: the contrast between what remains and what moves on, the tension between what was always there and the people who will someday have to leave and be left with nothing but their memories.

It had not been an easy road, to become a writer. He told us about the obstacles he faced, talking with the slight slur in syllables that discreetly characterizes almost all working-class Chilean males, while we all ate in that magical house where he lives with seven women—wife and daughters and a daughter-in-law and a granddaughter—painted blue like a ship in the middle of a barrio clinging to the steep slope that rises above Antofagasta.

Hernán had begun to write poems just after democracy was overthrown in 1973, paradoxically finding a slight voice of his own, just as the whole country was lapsing into silence and censorship—and the dictatorship might, in fact, have honed that voice of his by blocking him from early publication, helping him to avoid the trap of premature success that so many young writers fall into. The dictatorship—compounded by solitude. For years, he had no one to show his verses to except Mari, who encouraged him but had no literary interests whatsoever. In Pedro de Valdivia, Hernán would admire Professor Riquelme from afar, listening to his resonant voice and educated elocutions, and was tempted several times to show him his writings, but never dared. If he had even mentioned such a bizarre activity to the viejos, they might have mocked him. *Poesía es cosa de maricones,* poetry was supposed to be something for fags.... "They'd have started to grab my ass or something," Hernán said, smiling at Mari. "Not one person, in ten years, to talk about literature with. I didn't even know anyone who read, let alone wrote. I ended up reading my verses quietly to the books I'd take out of the library, reading to the great dead poets so they would keep me company...." It took him the seventeen years of the dictatorship to start writing his first novel, which he started in 1990—one could suggest when the country itself was readying itself to listen to the stories that had been suppressed for such a long period. Even so, it would take him many years to finish that novel—and he only did so once Pedro de Valdivia was closed down and the family was forced to move to Antofagasta. The loss of the pampa allowing him the pain and distance to tell its tale. The result was *La Reina Isabel Cantaba Rancheras*—which won one of Chile's major novelistic awards, sold tens of thousands of copies, and turned him into a public icon.

We had seen a display of the reverence he commands during our first night in Antofagasta, when we had a drink at the hotel bar. Though Hernán had never ventured into that hotel before that evening and knew no one there, the young waiter had not let us pay—"Sr. Rivera Letelier does not pay here," was the only explanation. A small gesture of acknowledgment from people who have read him or know of his books, perhaps the son of a *pampino* who wants to thank him for giving expression to that world of his forefathers. Hernán told us of other such incidents—the most recent when he had gone to see a friend at a hospital and been asked to look in on an extremely sick old man, who had started to cry and kiss Hernan's hand, assuring him he'd read every last book that hand had ever written and that now he was dying. And Rivera Letelier, incredibly moved, defended himself with a touch of irony: "Well, if you like my books so much, you'll have to wait a bit, you can't leave us now, because I am writing a book at the moment that's coming out just right." And two days later, the son of that man—a lawyer, elegantly dressed—stopped Hernán in downtown Antofagasta to thank him, because he had resurrected the old man, who was now back home, feeling much better and getting ready to read the newest book as soon as it was published.

I heard these and other anecdotes—women bringing babies for Hernán to touch, a resplendent feminine reader declaring her eternal love on her knees at a book fair—and see behind them something more than the hunger for stories in an age of oblivion and consumerism that Hernán seems to think is the primary reason for his widespread popularity. I had explained my theory to him last night, as we were about to depart after our meal, telling him that I thought people in Chile recognized in him the dream they themselves cannot see fulfilled, the working-class *calichero* who slipped away from the life of suffering and poverty that they continue to endure. Made all the sweeter by the fact that this escape has been master-minded using the magical power of the written word. People who write and read those messages of stone in the desert must see in him someone who has made good on the human promise not to let the past be lost forever.

At the door to his house, we had stopped. Below us the lights of the port of Antofagasta sparkled, making the ugly gray city down there almost look enticing.

"So what happened?" I asked.

"What happened where?"

"At Pampa Unión. When the train with the president pulled in? We're going to pass through there tomorrow, you know."

"Oh, yes. At exactly 3:08 in the afternoon the train pulls in. Everybody waits and waits, the Boy Scouts from the nearby towns, the Red Cross, the fire brigade, from every little hamlet, the basketball team, the soccer team. And the man who was going to make the speech clears his throat and gets ready to hand the president their petition to make them into a real and recognized locality and they keep on waiting while the locomotive is serviced. And then …"

"And then…?" Angélica asked.

"And then at 3:14 in the afternoon, the train pulls out of the station."

"No president."

"He did not even poke his head out a window…."

"As if they did not exist," I had said to him last night, I say to myself again as I contemplate the desolation in which the whorehouses of Pampa Unión now lie, that whole town built for no other purpose than for men to make love in the desert. "As if those people had never existed."

My mind still resonating with Hernán's answer.

"Except for me," Hernán had said to us last night, whispers to Pampa Unión today. "I'm here to tell their story."

Mountain of Fire

Friday, May 17, 2002. Chuquicamata.

I look around the giant dining room where we are eating a scrumptious Chilean lunch—shellfish and *congrio* eel and perfectly chilled white wine, talking about the production of copper at the largest open-air mine pit in the world, I look at the thirty, maybe forty tables with their red tablecloths and their crisp napkins on which hundreds of thousands of meals have been served, first to the Americans who owned this mine and since 1971 to the Chileans who nationalized it and took it over, I look past the adept waiters and the desserts and cake being lavished on the diners at other tables, out onto the looming mountain outside that will soon descend upon all of this, these lush chairs that we are all sitting on, these luxurious chandeliers that hang above us, yes, it is hard to believe that it will all soon be gone, that in one year's time this whole building with candelabra and kitchen and polished dark wooden walls and exquisite window work and the adjacent cafeteria that is serving food to 1,500 employees, I tell myself that it can't be true that this entire facility, and the town itself, which stretches out on all sides, with its streets, its hospitals, its police station, all, all of it, will lie beneath a colossal mound of *ripio*—rubble, yes, billions of tons of refuse from the mine of Chuquicamata, the largest industrial complex in the world, will cover the very spot where Angélica and I are being hosted by Coset Avalos and Orlando Nanjari Cortés, high-ranking executives of Codelco, la Corporación Nacional de Cobre de Chile.

Cobre.

After the nitrate bust drove Chile into near bankruptcy as a nation, it was copper that came to the rescue. That mineral, which shines with a lovely fiery red in its final, purified state, has been extracted by every population inhabiting the northern desert—manifold waves of Precolumbians, Spanish colonizers, *peruanos* and *bolvianos* and *chilenos* once their nations were independent—but it was only after 1910, when the Guggenheim company inaugurated this mine, refining the minerals of Chuquicamata with the same method that would be applied twenty years later to the nitrate of María Elena and Pedro de Valdivia, that copper was on its path to becoming the major export commodity of Chile. Today, my country provides 60 percent of the planet's consumption of copper and those overseas shipments account for 40 percent of the national budget, not as worrisome a dependency as in the times of nitrate, but still distressing. If some country or lab or mad genius discovered a substitute for copper, as one was found for the white gold of the *salitreras,* Chile's survival as a nation would be threatened.

Our hosts Coset and Orlando see no possibility of this happening—though, of course, that would have been the answer from any nitrate executive if I had popped him (no, there was no *her* back then) the question almost a hundred years ago. Weren't there rumors a while back that aluminum was going to crowd copper out of the market, that fiber optics was going to destroy copper's use in the informatics industry? And Orlando Nanjari Cortés responds that the contemporary world could not exist without what he calls "this most noble of metals." No airplanes, no cars, no computer chips, no cables. It is, he says, simply the best (and least expensive) conductor of electricity ever discovered.

And there is no chance, Coset Avalos adds, that Chile will ever run out of copper either, as new mines are being opened all over this part of the desert. We happen to be sitting on the richest mountain of copper that exists on the planet, churning out sixty thousand tons of pure mineral every day, and, in fact, the production in the mine of Chuquicamata will increase significantly once this town, popularly called Chuqui, is evacuated. Although the process of transferring its twelve thousand inhabitants has been expensive, the costs will be more than recovered by the profits accrued from the mine's expansion.

"Did you see the *tortas,*" Orlando asks, "when you drove up from Calama this morning?"

Indeed, it had been an amazing spectacle as we ascended those ten miles toward Chuqui, the road a straight line up and up the incline of the mount from the oasis town of Calama, where we had spent the night. As we approached the mine, we realized that what we had thought were natural hills sloping up and down the top of the ridge were, in fact, enormous knolls of rubble, tortas, monstrously immense cakes of dirt and refuse. So heavy that they were in danger of falling on the mine, crumbling inward, a Babel of stone and dust that threatens to destroy the industrial part of Chuquicamata. Instead, the billions of tons of debris will be emptied on the town. Humans, after all, unlike the mine, can be moved. Another advantage: the slag of each day, which in recent years the company has had to transport to dump ever farther into the desert—in trucks that guzzle two exorbitant liters of diesel per minute—will now be inexpensively filling up the hollow many miles wide where the town used to nestle.

Just as crucial are the environmental and health reasons. The industrial plant of Chuquicamata spews forth a vicious mix of dust, sulfur, and arsenic. So much arsenic, indeed, that a story circulates about a miner who died of a heart attack one night on a vacation in Madrid and whose wife was arrested by the Spanish police on the suspicion of having poisoned her husband. She was set free only after it was explained to the authorities that everybody who drinks for more than a year in the waters of Chuqui has enough arsenic in their veins to make an Agatha Christie detective green with envy.

Angélica and I could attest to the pollution plaguing the mine and its surroundings without—or so we hoped—having been poisoned. Last night we had received a call at our hotel in Calama from Patricio Hidalgo, the PR person who was to be our guide during our day in Chuquicamata, asking us to wear thick shoes and long trousers and long-sleeved shirts, though none of the clothes we finally sported were deemed to be protective enough. So Patricio had encased us in some dark blue padded rubber jackets, boots, red helmets, bloated goggles, and a breathing mask; and armed with this extensive shield against the depredations of the mine—minor apparel compared with the added gloves and flaps and sheaths that workers have to wear—we had set out to discover what it takes to make the copper that saves the Chilean economy, fuels the hospitals, pays for schoolteachers and libraries and sewers, paves the very road we took to the North.

Because copper cannot be exported until it is 99.7 percent pure, the mineral ore, once it is extracted and crushed into a size where it can be functionally handled, needs to suffer—I can think of no other word—a series of purgatorial burnings that purify the material over and over and over again.

This separation of copper from the other metals that have accompanied its existence up till then in the bowels of the mountain of Chuquicamata is achieved primarily by one element: fire. Not just ordinary fire. Fire such as I had never experienced before in my life. Fire that cooks the blood of those who do the work, cooks it slowly over the years until the blood no longer circulates as it should. Fire that first smelts the concentrate in enormous vats two stories high billowing smoke upward and outward and inward into our eyes and our lungs, making the atmosphere of that vast cavernous industrial plant murky and blurred. Fire illuminating the canyons formed by cauldron after cauldron, white-hot embers dribbling down to

Chuquicamata: Copper smelting

the ground where they form a paste of ashes and dregs over which tightly sealed vehicles roam, their lights switched on forlornly in the thick dim haze while above them red-hot claws as large as a horse move back and forth, back and forth. Fire roaring and hissing and trying to make itself heard above the buzzers and beeps and loudspeakers clamoring with incomprehensible warnings. And then fire again, when the lava of liquid copper as white as the sun at midday cascades from above into a sort of giant ladle that captures and cradles the flow and then pours it down into molds that have themselves been heated at searing temperatures in order to resist their incandescent cargo. And then, and only then, water. Water itself boiled blue with chemical agents—and yet so much cooler than the sheets and bars of copper that drown in it and are bathed and calmed in its tides, water from which fumes also emerge. And then and only then, after enduring, ourselves and the mineral ore, a second immense industrial warehouse—"like a vast indoor desert," Angélica had suggested—brimming with grills from which the sheets of copper hang, are we finally free to retreat into the open air to observe the end product. The marks of the fire barely on the surface of these bars that will soon be on their way to Antofagasta by the train we saw yesterday steaming through Pampa Unión. Whereas the most beautiful sheets of copper are rejected because of imperfections and nodules and tiny bubbles that would not allow electricity to course through it as required. All the colors that went into readying that copper blending into one another in those sheets like pictures lying in layer after layer in the sun waiting to be returned to the fire for another session of expurgation or simply cast aside, those flat images that, if I could take them to a museum, would be deemed works of maniacal genius. Only the copper that does not carry any blemishes, that has been wiped clean of what it went through, going off into the world to be used.

And we were able at last to hoist our goggles and lift our masks and breathe the air, which, Patricio Hidalgo informed us, is also contaminated.

"But one thing," he said, "is what we go through and quite another is our families. As workers, we have no alternative, we will always have a lower life expectancy than the average Chilean, but our folks can at least be removed from greater danger. We can't live at home with the kids, with our wives, using masks all day. Not easy to give the wife a good morning kiss."

Patricio was born in Chuquicamata, but realizes that, for his health and the health of everyone who works there as well as for the financial health of the company, his place of birth must be buried under a mountain of rubble, the whole area kept only as an industrial zone.

Not everybody turned out to be so understanding, we discover now at lunch with Coset and Orlando. Even Coset herself—who is in charge of explaining the eradication of the town of Chuqui to the outside world—lets certain misgivings seep into her conversation. She had one of the last babies delivered at the hospital here, right down the road. It no longer is in service, is being buried under a river of stones at this very moment that we sip our mint tea.

I feel strangely like a ghoul, intent on adding yet another version of ruin in the Norte Grande to my collection, perhaps unhealthily fascinated by the upcoming demise of the community that is having lunch all around us, in this dining room and down in the houses and restaurants of Chuqui itself. But it is such a perverse privilege, to be able to visit a town just before it becomes a ghost instead of wandering through it after it has been destroyed. Like visiting Pompeii the night before Vesuvius erupted.

"How do I tell my son where he was born?" Coset asks now. "How will he be able to imagine that place?" Though she does feel that she will be able to explain to him that this is already, after all, a tradition in their family, this loss of the hometown. Like so many of those who are now at Chuqui—and in what other school could they have learned how to endure that sort of work, that sort of heat, that sort of extreme exertion?—she comes from a family of *pampinos*. Her grandfather, in fact, had been born in Pampa Unión.

Pampa Unión?

We chat a bit about that center of damnation that we have passed through only yesterday. And Chuqui will also, after all, soon be like a village of the damned, is already about to graduate to that dubious status, except that here not even relics of walls will be left behind to remind visitors of past glories.

But Coset is quick to point out a more crucial distinction: that Chuqui is, in fact, the opposite of the Pampa Unión community, whose townsfolk were ignored by everybody with power. Authorities here do listen, have to listen, to those who will be affected by these decisions. As in the case of Soquimich, the company here, Codelco, owns everything in the township of Chuqui, from the land to the houses and services. But this is not María Elena, where the eviction was decided at the table I had sat at one day without any worker being present. Not only because this is state-run and therefore democratically accountable, but because copper's economic preeminence in the country has produced trade unions that are the strongest and most seasoned in Chile. They know and management knows that they can bring to a halt in a few hours what is still the bloodstream of the country. Over the years they have wrested all manner of extraordinary benefits from the company, and you can see the result merely by taking a walk, as we did last night, Thursday night, through the *paseo peatonal* Ramírez in Calama, where most of them live and where the rest of them will end up.

We brushed up against the most uniformly prosperous populace we had ever regarded in any corner of Chile—including the posh neighborhoods of Santiago. Not strange, given the high salaries for workers and employees in one of the most arid places in the world. What was jarring was how—dare I say it?—how Indian the inhabitants of Calama looked. In Latin America's racist societies, there may be some people with indigenous features and bronze skin who shop till they drop, but they tend to be a ripple in the ocean of an invariably larger dark majority who, near and far, are depressingly poor and wretched. Calama is how our Latino cities would look, should look, if the people who worked had excellent wages and services. It can indeed be held up, at least in this respect, as a model, a sort of Utopian metropolis. Though economic paradise for all has consequences, of course, as opulent cities all over the globe can testify. We found Calama already overcrowded, its streets choked full of cars (everybody owns a car, an astonishing situation in a Chilean town), and so we wonder aloud what will happen when the hordes of new inhabitants coming from Chuqui are squeezed into this ever diminishing oasis. In colonial times Calama, smack in the middle of the Río Loa, was the largest verdant area in the whole Norte Grande and is now losing trees and vegetable patches practically by the day. People gobble up the trendiest goods from around the world and wear the latest Nikes without seeming to be aware that unrestricted consumption of this sort could well lead to the consumers themselves being gobbled up by the desert—not that I am in any position to really launch this kind of critique, given that I enjoy in the United States a life of affluence and effluence that the men and women of Calama have as much right to as anybody else on this globe.

Orlando, at any rate, views the transfer of such a large population as an opportunity that he hopes will not be misused. He arrived here thirty-two years ago from La Serena with the intention, like so many who come to the desert, of staying a short while. Calama is now his home—but he recognizes that it was never able to grow as a community. It had an old history, but most of its inhabitants proceed from some other place, so it turned into a *ciudad dormitorio,* a satellite city, only for sleeping by night, sleepwalking by day. There's a chance, with all the money that will be invested in the near future, to change the mentality of its residents, build a mall, open a university, solve the traffic problems, leave a certain architectural mark on the land, forge a new identity.

"When I came here," Orlando says, "I didn't know anybody, not even a scorpion, not a snake. The Chilexploration Company still owned this mine. Maybe you saw the signs in English as you came in, maybe you noticed that some of them still say CHILEX."

I had, in fact, noted those signs—partly because I had invented in a novel a crazed dystopian country of the future I called Chilex, meaning ex-Chile, a country that was no longer Chile and where everything from the children to the orgasms were for export, not knowing that such a name had been branded on a real town and a real industry in the desert. But equally intriguing to me was the survival of those other signs in an English language that was as much my own as Spanish. Thirty or so years after nationalization took the mine away from the Americans, the original language they had brought with their capital and their machines to this mountain still persisted in warnings and signals and bathrooms and instructions, everything still measured in yards and miles and inches. But I do not interrupt Orlando's musings with my own bilingual or literary obsessions, at least not yet.

He tells us that only *pulperías,* company stores, were allowed in Chuqui when he first made this place his home, with no freedom, as there is now, for every major chain to open a supermarket. He tells us how the Americans not only were cut off from Chile (there was a single flight a week instead of today's dozen or so daily flights) but also made efforts to cut the Chilean technical staff off from the workers. This dining room, of course, was out of bounds to workers and most Chilenos, as was the giant pool, the bowling halls, the astounding bar. And when Orlando dropped in at the Club Obrero, the locale where workers got together to socialize in the evenings, the next day John Tucker, a top executive, warned him: "I don't want to see you going in there anymore." Orlando's protests that he was the owner of his own free time had been met by Tucker's response: "Well, you either stop going there or you look for a new job." Because if an engineer like Orlando mingled with laborers, he would lose his ascendancy over them and they, so the theory went, would lose respect for him.

Things had changed.

"Everything," Orlando says, "regarding the eradication process was consulted with the unions and they consulted everything with the workers. We have been negotiating, are still negotiating, every last detail and desire, from the color of the houses in Calama to the way in which the sports clubs will be built and where the teams will meet and practice."

I decide to test the limits of this nonauthoritarian process by posing a really troublesome question, one that I have, indeed, been asking all morning, getting a variably hesitant answer from each person I have met.

What about the cemetery? Will it also be buried in rubble?

Patricio Hidalgo said he didn't know, a worker with whom I managed to exchange some words told me the cemetery was untouchable and nobody would leave Chuqui unless its integrity was guaranteed, yet another shrugged his shoulders and said, with resignation, that the whole town was to be flooded with stones and that was that, *oleado y sacramentado*. And neither Coset nor Orlando seems to be able to give me a definitive answer—merely a puzzled "that is still being discussed." Though I have the feeling that Orlando may know something else. "It'll work itself out," he assures me as we all stand up at the end of lunch. "That issue will be fixed, as everything else has been, by consensus."

I let the question lapse as we say good-bye and head off to the last part of our tour, a visit to the mine itself, which is the source of all the wealth that feeds Chile and also the source of all the rubble that may or may not bury the graveyard where the living of Chuquicamata have been burying their dead for nearly a century.

I cannot know that I will only find the answer to that uncomfortable question about the dead of the town, only receive a real response this very night, on the other side of the mountains a hundred or so kilometers southeast of Chuqui, the answer will walk up to me in the most unlikely of places. I will be sitting in the restaurant La Estaka in San Pedro de

Atacama—that village where magical events happen, day after day, have been happening for centuries—when who will stroll in but Senator Ricardo Núñez, one of my university pals (from the time of Freddy Taberna), who represents this region and had been the one who, back in Santiago, arranged the Chuqui visit for us. He had originally suggested he might join our tour or perhaps our lunch, but he had been tied up in political meetings and had not been able to converge with Angélica and me. Knowing our schedule, he had decided to try and track us down over the weekend in San Pedro. One of the friends he had brought with him on that visit was none other than Juan Pablo Scroogie, the head lawyer of Codelco in the negotiations with the workers regarding the transfer of the townspeople of Chuqui to Calama. For over a year Scroogie not only led the public sessions, but also the more private and informal conversations where the real deals always end up being struck. "Codelco's mistake," Scroogie will tell me thirty-six hours from now, as he sips a pungent *pisco-sour*, "was to always suppose that the problem was money, money, always money, and that if you threw enough compensation at the workers, any obstacle could be overcome." He will look at the fire roaring away in one corner of the restaurant, our only shield from the cold mountain air pouring through the doors of La Estaka, a fire that may remind him, and will certainly remind me, of the furnaces of Chuqui all those miles away, burning night and day on the other side of the low mountain range both he and I have had to cross to get to San Pedro. "We brought money to the table," Scroogie will go on, "and each time the trade union representatives resisted, we kept offering more and more. But it wasn't a problem of numbers but a problem of culture. Three generations had been born, lived, and died there. It was the soccer club, it was the prom dance, it was where a man had first looked at the woman who would be his wife, it was where a kid had scraped her knee for the first time. So finally, when we started to offer to keep parts of old Chuqui alive, preserving this and that, the church, for instance, that's when we started to agree. And what was their first condition? The cemetery has to stay. The company has to keep it and upkeep it and provide a tomb to descendants of Chuqui families if they wish to be interred there. The clause we signed just a few days ago states that the cemetery is to keep on functioning as long as the mineral does not run out."

That is what he will tell me tonight about the dead of Chuquicamata.

As to the death of Chuquicamata itself, that is what I am to discover now, when Angélica and I visit, after lunch, the open pit itself. Here is where our tour ends, looking into the immense maw of an amphitheater of stone and slag, seven and a half kilometers long and four and a half kilometers wide and almost one kilometer deep. Far down below we can see gigantic shovel trucks (with tires three meters high that cost twelve thousand dollars each) excavating the terraces of material that have been dynamited from the rock this very morning. Ramón Morales, the electronic engineer in charge of security, tells us that there is a need to rein in those *tronaduras*—detonations, the English translation, does not contain the pregnant Spanish expression of *trueno,* thunder, or even the *dura* part, which echoes with hardness, something quite fatal and definite that cannot be softened by prayers or sacrifices. This mine has been suffering these discharges for eighty-seven years.... When Chuquicamata was young, people would come from near and far to watch the spectacle of millions of tons of material being blasted out of the womb of the mountain—somewhat in the way in which the public gathers in our cities to behold a building being demolished. Nowadays the violence performed on the mountain is more like surgery than the previous sort of butchery. The geologists operate carefully, very selectively, so that the resulting fractured components—no more than a meter and a half in diameter each—can fit in the crushing machines. More crucial, perhaps, is that they need to take into consideration the delicate architecture and condition of the mine—and I am struck by the way in which Morales refers to this open-air pit almost as if it were a sick patient.

And, in effect, he says, the mine is beginning to show cracks, it is beginning to ———

He stops and makes a large circular gesture. Every day 600,000 tons of material are extracted. One fourth of that, 150,000 tons, goes on for treatment in the mills and crushers and fires that await them further on. But the other three-quarters of what is taken from the earth end up as *lastre,* debris, and go to engross the tortas, which we can now see from the other side of the horizon, and which from here look more menacing than they did this morning as we cheerfully drove up from Calama, brooding plasters of rock thrusting upward and sideways, filled to capacity, threatening more than to overflow onto the nearby township. Because it is too much of a burden: The billions of billions of pounds are loaded like a curse of stone on the mine, weighing it down, encumbering its very existence.

Chuquicamata: The open pit copper mine

"We need to get at the richer ore that is below, ever deeper," says Morales. "And any child who is building a sand castle can tell you that you need to enlarge and expand above if you want to dig at the foundations below. " He points at a tremendous shovel slowly pushing back the upper eastern perimeter of the pit so it will not collapse onto the newer works. Widen above so that way down in the artificial valley— like the wound left by a mammoth comet—the removal and extrication of the mineral can continue ceaselessly. And on the opposite ridge, at the top of the west side, I see another couple of trucks pushing material outward. If I were to come back in forty years, the quarries will be there, fifteen to eighteen meters high just like now, and the greenish colors will indicate the presence of copper and the white ones will whisper that sulfur is mixed in waiting to find its dusty way into the air, everything like now, except the pit will be wider, longer, deeper—and still more arid.

"Does it matter to the mountain?" I suddenly ask Ramón Morales.

He is not taken aback at my anthropomorphization of Chuqui, though for the first time he does not answer immediately, takes his time. He has told us already of the accidents that happen from time to time no matter how cautious they are. I can see the same pain creeping into his eyes now that was there when a while ago he spoke about losing a miner, watching one of his men mutilated for life.

"Yes," he answers now, "I think it does matter to the mountain. The mountain knows its own history. How does it make us pay? *¿Cómo nos cobra?* In sicknesses, in men who die many years before they should, of silicosis, from other things. And we have a large quota of children born with deformities, leporine lips, cancers. Moving to Calama may help diminish the human cost but it will never go away entirely. Nature takes back in other ways what we are extracting from it. Collecting for what we did to it. You can't take from Nature and not pay the price."

I watch the dust rising from the mine into the clear wondrous sky of the desert and the small trucks following their mammoth fellow shovel trucks up the embankment, casting thousands of tons of water on the road to spare those expensive tires from wearing out, to spare our lungs from breathing in even more of this poisonous dead powder.

And I remember two indigenous legends about the origins of Chuquicamata.

One says that the gods gave men copper in abundance because they need something different from the gold and the silver that divides people and makes them envious and fight each other, men need a metal that can be mined only if everybody works together. And this is a legend that I can see at work today in this mine and the mines that have closed and, I suppose, in every mine that will ever open in this desert or any other desert in the world: The bonds forged by those who dare to take from the Earth what it may not want to give up.

The second legend recounts that the Great God of the coyas, Apu Punchau, had priestesses—daughters, others say—who served him as guardians, *ñustas* of his temple. Evil men came, searching for gold and treasures and plundered the sacred shrine and killed the maidens. Apu boiled over and dried up all the rivers and destroyed those men and swore that the blood of his beloved votaries would not be wasted. He made their souls into stars—three of them, the *yapus,* into the stars that form *las tres Marías,* the three Marys, and the ñusta Inti, who was the loveliest and whitest of them, into the *lucero,* the star of the morning. But when he squeezed their heart to forge them into stars, the blood spilled over the zone that was Chuqui and he proclaimed that each drop of their blood would be turned into wealth for the men who would someday come to inhabit these lands. A variation of the legend, perhaps a modern one, adds that Apu's wrath is remembered by the land each time that the mountain explodes and thunder rolls from it.

Looking at the open pit of Chuquicamata, which in a few hours' time will once again, as in the last eighty-seven years, suffer yet another and another and another blast, each one equivalent to a magnitude five earthquake on the Richter scale, thinking about the endless tronaduras during endless tomorrows, I am not sure—who could be?—if Apu and the other gods anticipated what men would do when they came to extract the mineral, I am not sure if he and the others will be as benevolent with us next time, if next time around we will be this lucky.

Under the Sand

Saturday, May 18, 2002. San Pedro de Atacama.

We are standing, Lautaro and Carolina and Angélica and me, on a windswept dune a few miles from San Pedro de Atacama, a lovely oasis that humans had been inhabiting for many millennia before Pedro de Valdivia passed through in 1540 on his way southward to conquer what even then was called Chile; we have come to watch the sun set on this specific spot in the desert of Atacama, because under the sand at our feet, according to Lautaro Núñez, Chile's preeminent archaeologist, there lies the village of Beter, a *Pueblo de Indios* built by the Spanish in the seventeenth century to seclude and tax the descendants of those humans who had hunted and farmed and baked pottery in this valley for thousands and thousands of years.

We could be visiting other ruins, ruins that are, at least, visible. We could be climbing up the fortifications at Quitor, on a hill not far from here, where the Indians made a stand against Valdivia's horses and clanging warriors and met a terrible defeat. We could be drinking in the last rays of the sun from the top of that twelfth-century Pukará fortress where three hundred native chiefs had their heads chopped off after they surrendered. Or we could be wandering farther up the gorge of the Río San Pedro among the remains of Catarpe, from where the Incas had administered these lands when they arrived in 1450 and where we might get some sense of how the residences were constructed, have some hint of human habitation. Or better yet, on our way to the amazing rock statues of the Valle de la Luna at the far entrance to this valley, we could have stopped by Tulor, dating from eight hundred years before Christ, where the sand has been partly brushed away from the circular remains of the oldest village ever discovered in the area, whose curators are the Indians of Coyo, who cultivate the plush nearby fields. Or if we wanted to call on some of the other *ayllus,* the indigenous communities that cultivate every inch of this sprawling oasis, we could get there by driving up once again through the Valle de la Muerte, the Valley of Death that we have had to cross to arrive in San Pedro, we could tarry by that flank of immense, foreboding crags that brood over the road as if they were tutelary statues, guarding these lands from foreign eyes, brooding over a past that only they have seen.

But my old friend Lautaro—I am amazed at how time has hardly changed him since I saw him last, only the silver hairs

San Pedro de Atacama: Lautaro Núñez at a Pueblo de Indios

in his beard suggesting forty years have passed, still possessed by the same mouselike energy and agitation that earned him his nickname of *Laucha*—has insisted that we make a pilgrimage to the Pueblo de Indios, and it is useless to argue with him or with Carolina Agüero, who has also enthusiastically endorsed his suggestion. And who to trust in these matters if not her, the only archaeologist in our extended family, still considered a relative by us even if her brother Nacho is no longer married to Angélica's sister, still the aunt of our darling nieces in Santiago, who have kept tabs on our expedition, who keep calling us on the road to send love to Tía Carolina. Though both Angélica and I would probably have come to San Pedro de Atacama anyway, famed for its lovely adobelike houses and stately ancient trees and perfectly white colonial church, we firmed up plans only once we realized that Carolina was installed here permanently and that Lautaro was going to drive up from Antofagasta, where he lives half the week, to spend these days with us. We've just had a lengthy and raucous lunch at his home here in San Pedro, where everything is so archaeological and brimming with the past that when he was extending one of the walls of the house, he discovered in the garden the mummy of an Indian. Lautaro calculated where the man came from (the other side of the cordillera in what was then not yet called Argentina), what his profession was (to trade and acquire), what funeral rites were appropriate given his age (he'd died sometime in the vicinity of A.D. 800), and invited friends and colleagues to a dinner in the dead man's honor and reburied him with all his objects and all the respect he was due. It may have been the recounting of that incident—or perhaps it had been in Lautaro's mind all afternoon—that made him stand up suddenly from the table, gesture toward the sun that was looping downward and the wind that was blowing up a storm of sand and propose that we visit Beter, where, he promised, nobody ever goes.

He is right. There is not a tourist in sight. But neither is there a ruin to be photographed, not an intimation of a human dwelling place, though now, as we step through the brush, we begin to discern some stones jutting up in an orderly fashion out of the sands, what used to be, Carolina says, the roof of a house that is waiting to be dug up if funds ever materialize, and there, farther on, what looks like a cross is peeking out of the earth and that marks where the only whites lived, the priests sent by the Crown to christianize the Indians. This was the policy of Viceroy Toledo in the seventeenth century—to segregate the native population from the Spanish and mestizos in a sort of apartheid of the time, erect villages where they could be more easily indoctrinated and controlled and made to work. "There," says Lautaro, pointing to a dune overgrown with bracken, "next to the *capilla* was the cemetery—turned into the only escape route to heaven, administered by the evangelizers. And the plaza directly in front of it. Everything traced on the Spanish model—except the only residents allowed were Indians—and their holy foreign fathers."

The town that is deep down there, several meters under our shoes, its web of streets barely discernible as we walk over them, was conceived as the twin to San Pedro itself. All over the Norte Grande, in each oasis, you can distinguish two communities, one next to the other, like Pica and Mantilla or San Lorenzo de Tarapacá and Huarasí. Except that those other Pueblos de Indios were not abandoned like this one was, they do not expose life as it used to be back then, at the crucial moment in the history of Latin America when the colonizers and the conquered were beginning to establish what would be their common culture.

"If we excavate here," Carolina explains, raising her voice so the hoarse wind will not drown her out, "we'll find ceramic remnants that come from the indigenous tradition and also ceramics that are entirely Spanish as well as objects where both traditions have merged and created a syncretic mix."

Lautaro nods his head and adjusts his ever present beret so the wind will not blow it away. He has explained, this afternoon, that the whole history of Chile is spun as a military epic, an incessant war of conquest on the part of the invaders or of resistance on the part of the natives, which is basically true of the South of the country, where the Mapuches held out against the Spanish almost till the end of the nineteenth century, but there is another, perhaps more exciting story that can be unearthed in a place like this Pueblo of Indios that we are now visiting. All it would take is to dig just a bit and bones of animals and feathers of poultry and residues of eggshells would be disclosed, reminders that the conquistadores came not only with the sword and the cross but also with the chicken. In Beter, for instance, the Indians were forced to cultivate wheat, a European crop that would feed those engaged in mining in the outlying areas—but the agricultural implements they used had been manufactured using pre-Columbian smelting techniques. Which means that life was forged in that day-to-day crucible of the seventeenth century out of a slow coexistence of two cultures rather than a collision, subtly haggling with each other over what was going to be used from their respective traditions, what would remain, what would change.

And it is in the desert, in this driest of dry dwelling places, that these and so many other secrets of the past can be uncovered because, quite simply, in a place like this they have never been truly lost. They have merely been waiting for the right hand, the right eye, the right questions, to bring them back to life.

It is a task to which Lautaro has dedicated his life, and the desert has been one of his main allies in the most difficult resurrection of them all, the attempt to rescue the story of the many migrations of indigenous men and women who came to the mesetas, valleys, and oases of the North in successive waves over the last eleven thousand years and created here a variety of civilizations of ever increasing complexity, culminating in the Atacameño culture, which has put San Pedro on the archaeological map of the world. Along with a group of other historians and archaeologists, Lautaro has been trying to establish the outlines of a chronology of the native inhabitants of the vast meseta that stretches to the south and north of San Pedro. To achieve this understanding does not merely fulfill an obligation to the dead and break down the silence to which they have been banished, but has consequences for the living. There are lessons that the desert can teach us if we only know what to seek, if we only give ourselves the opportunity to ask the questions that the men and women who originally thrived here found answers to, if we allow ourselves to be inspired, Lautaro suggests, by how the indigenous populations of the distant past, with fewer resources at their disposal than we have today, were able to solve problems posed to them by a bleak and apparently inhospitable environment. Like many other intellectuals and activists I have encountered across the globe who are engaged with what have been called "traditional communities," Lautaro believes that those ancestors of ours can spur us to rethink our social and economic development, find ways that would encourage contemporary people with scant means and assets to also defeat poverty, also harness technology to real human needs. Following the example left behind by those men and women long ago.

The civilizations that flourished in this region saw the desert in a very different manner than we do, with our emphasis on a relentless extraction of minerals and hardly any interest in the ecological consequences emanating from that relentlessness, our almost criminal indifference to the human suffering that such a process engenders. Without overidealizing the Indians, Lautaro and his colleagues think that those original settlers of this part of the Americas were able to understand the desert as an array of contrasting and complementary environments. If you travel from east to west, he says, from the peak of the Andes to the coasts of the Pacific, in those three hundred kilometers you will go from polar chills to tropical temperatures. The diversity of environments offers a diversity of resources—trees, fish, streams, orchards, minerals—a whole world concentrated in this part of America, a mosaic where every possibility of production is there, waiting. Waiting but hidden.

"The forest," Lautaro had said at our prolonged lunch, "does not present itself as it does in the Amazon. You have to ask the land how to make the trees that used to grow here grow again, the thousands of acres of *tamarugos* which were cut down and burnt for fuel. The lakes are here in the highlands, just above San Pedro and throughout the Andes, but we haven't asked them what sort of life they can sustain. All we do is drain their depths to send water to the mines and the ports that export what the mines yield. And the sea is there but we haven't asked it how we could create marine farms in it, just like we have agricultural farms on land. And don't get me started on solar energy and wind energy, which the Indians also knew so much about, which they used, in fact, to refine copper."

The questions have not been asked, according to Lautaro, because when a crisis arises in Chilean society, there has always been some mineral there, silver at first and then nitrate and now copper, that allows those in power a relatively exuberant lifestyle and hides those questions, in a sense, hides the mirror Chile needs to hold up to the face of the desert so that desert will cease to be an enigma.

It is for me a revelatory experience to spend these two days with Lautaro exploring this quest of his. I am reminded of our fleeting conversations forty years ago in the gardens of the university campus in Santiago where we both studied. It was Freddy Taberna, our friend executed in Pisagua in 1973, who brought us together back in the early sixties and who, I am convinced, has guided us toward this new meeting, as if he were interweaving the strands of his friends from beyond death. Freddy's wife, Jinny, had insisted that I speak to Lautaro before visiting Iquique, the city where both he and Freddy had been born and on whose streets they had first crossed paths. Lautaro had not only written a short and fervent book about Freddy's life and death but had also participated in the search for his body. "I never thought," Lautaro confided to me, once I had broached the subject this afternoon, "when I decided to go into archaeology, that the techniques I learned in order to detect the remote past I would someday have to employ to look for the bones of one of my dearest buddies. And I'm not the only one—ask any archaeologist or anthropologist in Chile. Every one of them has probably spent some time searching for the remains of former classmates and friends disappeared during the dictatorship."

That had certainly not been in his plans or on his mind— or mine, for that matter—when we ardently discussed the future of Latin America in our university days. I had been shaped, along with Lautaro and Freddy and a host of other young men and women of the time, by the intellectual upheaval of the sixties that demanded an alternative interpretation of history from this part of the world, and we had each gone forth to seek that history and become part of it. The paradox was that, fascinated as we were with the origins of our continent and its underdeveloped miserable present-day conditions, we cared to know next to nothing about the personal lives of those *compañeros,* friends and colleagues, with whom we were to undertake that mission. When you are young and the planet seems on the verge of burning down, it doesn't seem to matter much where you are coming from, may even be unable to recognize what deeper impulses from your own past quietly whittle and motivate your behavior. So I did not know then— or thought of asking—anything about the hidden sources of Lautaro's personal obsession with unearthing the past. I did not know about his indigenous great-grandmother or his Spanish ancestors who had settled in the Pica oasis back at the end of the sixteenth century in order to produce wine for the mine of Potosí, the largest mountain of silver ever discovered in the history of the world. I did not know how nitrate had determined his destiny even before he was born. I did not know how his family had been displaced from their farm in the Quisme oasis because their water had been channeled off to a thirsty and nitrate-bloated Iquique or how his Peruvian grandfather had been deported to Lima in the ethnic cleansing that the Norte Grande endured when the Patriotic Leagues organized by the Chileans had terrorized citizens who might support Peru's attempt to reclaim the lands lost in the War of the Pacific, the war over control of the *salitreras* and their wealth. I did not know that one of his earliest school memories would be a hunt for bones in the patio of the Escuela Santa María, his school in Iquique, where back in 1907 three thousand salitre workers and their wives and children had been massacred by the army when they had marched on Iquique to demand a living wage. I did not know that he had become an archaeologist because of Bertie Humberstone, the son of Santiago Humberstone, the British chemist who has applied the Shanks system to refine the salitre of the pampas, I did not know that it had been Bertie who invited Lautaro, then a child of nine, to come and join another group of boys who were receiving after-school lessons in the Humberstone household in Iquique, Bertie who first talked to him about the pyramids of Egypt and how this other desert, the desert out there that Bertie had been born in and then had left to be educated in England and had finally returned to once his university studies were over, that other nearby desert also had treasures and mysteries to be disinterred. So much that I did not know about Lautaro back then and that I had to come all the way to San Pedro de Atacama to discover, here, at this crossroads of the civilizations of the Andes where cultures and stories have been traded, first by the Atacameños and then by the Incas and later by so many others, the Spanish intent on their gold and the merchants from Bolivia and the cattle drivers from Argentina bringing meat to the *salitreras,* all of them passing through this oasis, as I was now, on their way to somewhere else.

Yes, this flowering junction in the desert had turned out to be a good place to meet up with Lautaro again, find out that the years of absence had only drawn us closer to each other, that we had matured in similar ways and with parallel obsessions.

And also, this interlude in the *precordillera* of San Pedro, apparently off our prescribed route of ghost towns, was proving to be a canny way of preparing for the more personal turn that this trip of ours is about to take, as we approach the Iquique where Angélica's ancestors came from, where Freddy lived his last years, where we will be sleeping tomorrow night. Where we will have to do what we have just done with Lautaro: start sweeping away the dust and rubble under which the past has been buried, each human being, after all, not that much different from this Pueblo de Indios that the sand has covered and whose real story can only be guessed at from the turrets and stones that surface out of the desert while the nearby volcanoes look on and do not speak. Is that why Lautaro wanted to bring us here, because this buried town symbolizes in some way what his life has been about, what he still needs to accomplish, all the secrets the Norte Grande is still waiting to reveal.

Secrets that he is not alone in exploring. No desert syndrome of loneliness seems to bedevil the small frame and enormous ambitions and boundless energy of Lautaro Núñez. A whole new generation of historians, anthropologists, and archaeologists are flocking to this region to try to explore the remote yesterdays that Lautaro and others like him have been mining as if they were nitrate or gold or copper. Carolina Agüero is, in fact, a prime example—one of Lautaro's many disciples.

Yesterday, the Friday we had arrived, and then again this morning we have been able to spend some nice hours alone with our relative wandering the dusty, narrow streets of San Pedro and, in my case, getting an exclusive tour of the museum that is the pride of this town (Angélica prefers to explore the church, talk to some of the townspeople). The museum houses almost four hundred thousand pieces culled from the surrounding desert by a Belgian father, Gustave Le Paige, who had come here in 1955 to serve as the local priest of what was then an even smaller community, and had dispensed the next thirty-five years of his life collecting bones and artifacts, pottery and tapestries. It was because of Le Paige's extraordinary and groundbreaking discoveries—particularly some mummies thousands of years old—that San Pedro was officially designated the archaeological capital of Chile.

Carolina had ended up in this oasis by accident—though she agreed with me when I interposed that nothing in life is really an accident—when she reluctantly accepted the post of resident archaeologist in San Pedro and spent the next couple of years certifying that the new roads being built to accommodate a recent and prodigious increase in tourism were not going to destroy any indigenous ruins. A feisty, high-spirited woman, she fought against the public works engineers, against the developers—and even against the army regiment, whose local commander had insisted that he had the right to indiscriminately shell any place in the desert he so desired, even if it meant targeting and blowing up ancient indigenous sites. When her time was up, she had left for London, where a loving boyfriend had been patiently waiting for the past two years and where she fully intended to pursue her doctoral studies. On the way back to Santiago—a quick trip to say good-bye to the family and pack her things before heading off to England again—something had awoken her in the middle of the night. There, stretched out in three seats in economy class, with the deep Atlantic below her and nothing but water for thousands of miles in any direction, she had suddenly said to herself, "I have to go back to the desert, back to San Pedro. That's where I'm needed, that's my destiny." And managed to secure a job as a researcher at the museum.

I asked her what I have been asking just about everybody I meet who has journeyed to the desert for what they think will only be a while and then stayed on. Why? What could possibly attract you to such a barren place?

Carolina recognized how difficult, how belligerent this environment can be. "The landscape," she said, "refuses to recognize you, *se te niega el paisaje,* but that very resistance gives you a chance, almost demands it, to find what is inside, to search for your own intimate warmth. There are no distractions, no facile alternatives—so you have to look for who you really are." She also understood this return as staking an identity, saw this, she said, as a way of redeeming her native heritage, a claim that surprised me. I have been close to her brother Nacho for several decades, as well as his twin, Felipe, and never once guessed that they might have the slightest drop of indigenous blood, seeming to be entirely European, a cross between the Agüero Spanish stock with the Polish Piwonkas. Carolina insisted that a branch of the Agüeros had originally settled not far from here, in Coyo, and that she could verify an Indian genealogy in the family. "Anyway," she added, "more than ethnic or racial traits, what determines your identity is what you do with your life, where you feel you belong." So she sees herself less as a foreign colonizer than as someone who has returned after centuries to what used to be the center of the world, her life a link to its original inhabitants. And her research is, in some way, the prolongation of that idea of San Pedro as an autonomous center in Andean prehistory rather than on the margins as it has often been portrayed. What she is trying to prove is that the history of this oasis cannot be understood as the result of the dominion of the great highland civilization of Tiawanaku, but that the people here developed a complex social and cultural organization almost entirely on their own.

Suddenly Carolina veered onto another, more contemporary and urgent subject. She stopped in front of a glass display case, in which the museum's most famous resident was crouching, an exquisitely preserved mummy of a woman dubbed by the local wags as "Miss Chile," perhaps as a way of exorcising that dead body or perhaps a reference to her utter nakedness, the way in which she was at the mercy of our stares and our curiosity. In fact, Carolina had informed me, a small group of San Pedro citizens had been denouncing that intolerable desecration of the *abuelos,* the grandfathers of Atacama, by the museum and demanding that they be returned to the earth. These insistent appeals, Carolina continued as we went on to view yet another mummy, were no laughing matter. There had been death threats. And a messianic Indian-rights movement had sprung up, claiming to represent the dead—even though most of its proponents had no idea whatsoever of how those dead had lived or how they had organized their everyday existence, something the archaeologists were patiently trying to reconstruct and understand. Remote ideological cousins of the murderous Sendero Luminoso guerrillas of Peru, attempting to revindicate the false authenticity of a past utopian era that cannot be brought back and that never, in fact, existed in the pure form that they propose, this clandestine band had recently unleashed a wave of violent assaults on what they considered the symbols of the Spanish usurpers. Last October 12—coinciding with the Columbus Day anniversary—they had tried to burn down the church and its saints—whose origins were, Carolina explained, less European than popular and indigenous. The proof was in the old men and women crying at the feet of the saints that had been burnt, caressing them, these images that had healed their children and helped to grow their crops. It was Carolina's job to write a report on the damage, and it broke her heart, she said, to see San Pedro—she means the statue, of course—with only a foot left jutting out of the charred remains of his body, a foot lovingly clothed in cotton sandals.

And then arsonists had tried to burn down the museum this last February 12—the emblematic day when Santiago had been founded by Pedro de Valdivia—and had not succeeded only due to what everyone declares was a miracle. Well, not everyone. The local fire brigade had volunteered a more rational diagnosis of how the museum had been saved: The flames had died down by themselves due to lack of sufficient oxygen. But that was not what the people of San Pedro believe. Persistent rumors circulate that *las momias soplaron,* the mummies, had breathed deeply and blown air in the direction of the fire and smothered it. The mummies, people were saying, had saved themselves and the artifacts. The mummies had made it clear that they did not want to be destroyed one more time, that they wanted the future to rescue them from oblivion.

I mention this to our friends now as the sun sinks below the horizon on this Saturday evening, as we bid farewell to the Pueblo de Indios. Carolina laughs. "That's what we need now," she says, as we head off to her house for dinner. "We need the mummies to come and blow the sand away, leave Beter as it once used to be, each house standing…. A real treasure of a village waiting, waiting. But the mummies had better hurry. Since the last time I came here, the sand has covered even more stones, you can see less and less with each visit."

Later at night, after Carolina has returned us to our Hotel Don Tomás in her Jeep, I switch on my mini-tape recorder in order to transcribe some of the words that our friends shouted our way in the Pueblo de Indios. It is almost impossible to hear anything. The wind has blown into the machine, crackled away the voices and hidden them in another sort of sand, almost as if the static were of sand rather than sound. Eerie and disturbing, I think to myself, given that our conversation in that ghost town was about the difficulties of mining the past, gently retrieving what it hides. As I fruitlessly try to listen and bleed some meaning from that most recent event, I cannot shake the impression that the wind does not want me to hear even the explanations of what might have happened in that place.

And of course there is one spot—there had to be, wouldn't there?—where I can catch a long moaning noise that does not seem to be the wind at all, but that sounds more like human wailing, a gathering of ghosts that has used this machine to allow us to faintly hear what our ordinary human ears are unable to perceive on their own.

Maybe this is what has been calling to Lautaro since he was a child and knew he would work in the desert to unearth its secrets, maybe this is what woke Carolina up in the middle of the Atlantic Ocean and forced her to change her destiny, maybe the real reason that Angélica and I needed to come to San Pedro de Atacama was to listen to what those voices are trying to say to us and that we still cannot understand.

THIRD PART: BODIES

Preservation Blues

Thursday, May 23, 2002. Santa Laura and Humberstone.
Outside Iquique.

I am standing where Julio Valdivia once danced as a young man over fifty years ago, here in the inner patio of the only residence left intact in the ghost town of Santa Laura, I am standing next to seventy-four-year-old Julio Valdivia, who is telling me about this place where he used to live and work and dance.

He had been given a room here for three months, Valdivia says to me and Senén Durán, the other member of this expedition, given a room in what was then the Casa de Administración, where employees were lodged while waiting for more permanent residence. "Here's where I slept, here's where my bed was and there was a dresser over there and look, here's where I could hang my clothes at night," he says, gesturing inside an airless chamber where only a dirt floor and a boarded window greet him now, all so different from when he had arrived in 1951 to start his job as an assistant in the *pulpería*, the company store.

We walk through the building—"Look, over there was the bathroom, look, over here is where we ate our dinner"—which now serves as a sort of impromptu display gallery, full of trinkets and mementos and old photos, set up by the mayor of nearby Pozo Almonte, who decided a few years ago to hire a guard to protect the site from thieves, explains Senén Durán, who heads a program at the university in Iquique that trains tourist guides and knows more about life in the pampa than anyone else I have met so far.

"Lucky for us the mayor acted like that, even if he did not have the legal right to do so," says Julio Valdivia, "or not even this might be left standing." In effect, every other house in Santa Laura has been torn down, its wood and tin dismantled over the years and sold for scrap by the Andía family, which acquired this *salitrera* and the other similar towns that made up the Cantón Nebraska in 1961, the year after they were all closed for good. What its erstwhile owners did not ever manage to find a buyer for was the *planta industrial,* which awaits our visit looming immensely a few hundred yards away, the only extant and almost flawlessly preserved example of how nitrate was refined with the Shanks system. This makes Santa Laura, with its machines and vats and enormous chimney thrusting up into the sky, an absolutely unique place in the whole *pampa salitrera.* And a perfect complement to the neighboring nitrate town of Humberstone, once the largest such community in the Norte Grande and that has kept all its streets

Santa Laura: An abandoned production facility

and residences, its theater and church and stores, almost exactly as they were the day it ceased to function over forty years ago, lacking only the factory building and industrial installations that can be found at Santa Laura. So between the two of them, these towns separated only by a few kilometers offer visitors a glimpse of what life must have been like during the nitrate boom. As long, of course, as Santa Laura and Humberstone continue to be preserved and do not end up like Oficina Alemania or Pampa Unión or any of the hundreds of abandoned and plundered sites we have passed in the desert. As long as people like Julio Valdivia and Senén Durán are successful.

They are the two most active members of the Corporación Museo del Salitre Humberstone-Santa Laura, a cultural foundation set up at the end of 1997 in order to save these two sites from being destroyed. It has taken the 1,500 members of the *corporación* almost five years to see their dreams begin to come true. Helped and inspired by my friend Sergio Bitar—the same former senator who organized my visit to María Elena and my encounter with the *pampinos* in Antofagasta, and who has also made it possible for me to spend some time with Julio Valdivia in Iquique—the Salitre Museum finally managed to buy Santa Laura and Humberstone at a public auction held in bankruptcy proceedings in March 2002. "Sergio Bitar is the one who found the money, working tirelessly," Julio had told me yesterday during a long afternoon at his home in Iquique, "but he wanted me, a real *pampino,* to be the one who called out the price. I lifted my hand up when the judge asked the future proprietor to speak out, I'm the one who said, here I am and here are the 120 million pesos, I'm the one who signed the legal papers in the name of us all, the thousands and thousands of men and women who gave us their signatures so the foundation could be legally recognized by the government. Every Sunday we would stand outside the station in Iquique, outside the churches in every town left in the pampa, outside the movie theaters, on the beaches, gathering signatures. So Sergio Bitar wanted us to be the owners of the oficinas where we used to work and live."

And now the hard part begins. They have to restore the *salitreras,* paint the houses, plant trees, hire guards, reintroduce electricity and running water, make sure the buildings are safe and secure for the tourists who, in recent years, have slowly started to trickle in to visit the towns. And the next phase will be to place markers and explanatory signs, install bathrooms and an administrative office, contract guides and build a camping site. It is in order to oversee all of this that Julio Valdivia will be moving to Humberstone in a few days' time, settling into a house that is being specially reconditioned to accommodate him, that should, in fact, be ready today for his inspection—which is the primary purpose of this trip that I have tagged on to. I am here, therefore, at a singular moment in the history of these ghost towns and of Julio Valdivia himself: when Humberstone will once again, after more than four decades, greet a permanent resident, the moment when Julio will return to live in the pampa that he was forced to leave when the *salitrera* of Victoria closed in 1980. I asked him about his wife and he responded, in a matter-of-fact tone of voice, that she would call on him from time to time, but basically she intended to stay behind in Iquique, where she had lived for most of her life anyway. "That's how it's been with us," Julio said. "There was no alternative. The desert demanded it. The money was there in the pampa, the education was here in Iquique. So the woman educated our five kids and I brought home the money. And now I have a mission, something I have to do before I die, and I am going to do it."

When he had stated that yesterday, so calm and obstinate, I felt that I was catching a glimpse of the sort of pioneering tenacity that had originally gone into colonizing this desert in the times of the nitrate boom, that a similar determination must have inspired the men who had set up the first stakes in Santa Laura in 1872. But it is only now, accompanying him as he walks through Santa Laura itself, that I can also sense the tenderness underlying his crusade, how he cares for this lost land as if it were a dying child in need of resuscitation. Through his eyes I watch the town begin to materialize again. But he is not strolling only through the past, but into the future as well, walking inside the plans for Santa Laura that he has begun hatching with Senén Durán. Listening to them is like eavesdropping on a couple of mischievous boys playing with a gigantic abandoned town, old Julio and middle-aged Senén conspiring about what to do here in what used to be the infirmary, how to restore that part of the *maestranza* over there.

Over there.

That is what keeps coming out of Julio Valdivia's mouth. Look, over there is where we had the soccer field and we brought the Colo-Colo professional club from Santiago to play a game. Look, over there is what we called *la casa de los secretos,* the house of secrets, because the chemist had forbidden any of us to enter or intrude and we wondered what he was mixing in his lab. Look, over there is the mechanical *taller* where the Sordo Romero—he was old and he was deaf—used to work. Over there was the hospital where Julio's son Chato was born. And here's where Miguel Barrera Solar would ring the bell to announce that the *suple* had arrived, the workers could get an advance on next week's salary. And those four steps, that was the theater. And here is where a man—Julio can't recall the name—came all mangled from an accident, he came here and his legs had been torn off *and there was nothing we could do for him.*

Julio speaks as if to himself. "*Se tronaba a las 11:30 de la mañana.* At 11:30 every morning they'd blast with dynamite and when it was ready, everyone would shout *Con Fuego,* It's on Fire—and the workers had to run as far and as fast as they could, hide wherever they could. Yeah, that's how things were. But at times it didn't explode—it was a *tiro echado,* the TNT hadn't gone off. So someone would have to go and check it out—and then it might detonate anyway.... Who was it, what was the name of that man who came with his stomach ripped open...?"

We do not answer. I was not there and Senén was not there and all around us are ruins, debris, chaff, dust, not an echo of the bell that Miguel Barrera Solar once rang in the quiet air of the afternoon of Santa Laura.

While Julio was describing to us the detailed map of the place that was still stirring in his head, while we tried to conjure up from his words what might have happened right here, I was reminded of a story that Lautaro Núñez had told me about a woman who had a surname something like Steen. Or was it Comber? Like Julio Valdivia, I am not sure about all the names of the people I am trying to evoke. At any rate, this Mrs. Steen, an extremely wealthy English lady now living in Sevilla, had been born in a pampa town and had, a few years ago, brought her grandchildren to the North of Chile. "Here is where I danced for the first time, look, look, this is where they handed me my first drink in life, so cold because they would bring the ice from the cordillera to cool off the gin and gin with which we celebrated Queen Victoria's birthday; and here is where my mother bought me the most gorgeous dress; and here is where we would cheer—in English!—the regattas in an artificial lake someone had built in the desert; and here is where we ate Bavarian ham with truffles from Tuscany brought in for the occasion," that is what she said to her descendants, according to Lautaro, and she would wave her arms and there was nothing there, just broken-down houses and scattered stones and refuse, nothing but the desert and yet more desert, and she had danced, a ninety-year-old woman dancing in the ruins. Lautaro was trying to convince her to write a book called *Estábamos Todos Locos,* We Were All Crazy— which would rescue life in the pampa from the forgotten point of view of the foreigners who had come to the desert at the pinnacle of its prosperity.

I am getting something just as hallucinatory from Julio Valdivia—though he is able, at least, to show me something more than the sand that the supposed Mrs. Steen had offered to her foreign family. *Here's where the band would play on Saturday and Wednesdays, can you believe that we used to pay them to play extra for us, so we could dance—yes, there were some single women around, the* libretera *who kept accounts and contracts and debts, the* cajera *who worked the cash register, the* tiendera *who waited on customers, and the three* empaquetadoras. *Five women at the* pulpería. *And the two who weren't married would come to dance. Don't get any wrong ideas. They slept in a different facility. María and Iris ... they had a grand time .... Out of our own pocket, we paid the band. We'd dance behind the* glorieta, *over there.*

And his stream of words ends with his finger pointing to a field of broken stones and grit, but there is a gazebo that I can see, something for me to fix on, bite into, as the film in his head continues to roll, images from the past flickering on the screen of his mind, superimposed on the ravaged present. It is all alive around him, the town and the people and the voices and the celebrations, a parade that none of his visitors would ever be able to really picture.

"Oh, you can't imagine what this was like," he says, "when the sun started to go down and the women were walking, swaying down the streets, and the kids would come out to play under the breeze as it freshened."

Now we have come to the company store where Julio Valdivia worked, the one business in the pampa that was always more profitable than the sale of nitrate itself, even in 1951 when tokens were no longer in use. In fact, yesterday afternoon at Julio Valdivia's house, he'd mentioned the name created by the *pampinos* to refer to the employees at the company store: *ratoneros,* because, like rats, they scrounged and hoarded. And stole from the customers. "Every kilo was always 800 grams," Julio had told me yesterday. "But we also performed an important service. The workers had no other place from which to buy."

It is a large area he is showing me: the *carbonera,* where they accumulated coal for sale. And the *carnicería.* And the *panadería. Look, over here was a bodega and we had grapes and lettuce and—look, out there, that was where the school was, right behind the store.* Again, there is nothing there—we peer through emptiness at a field where only shards of glass remind us that this was more than a desert, that this place was once inhabited.

"This is where Don Victor Núñez Acuña, the *administrador,* would begin his walk to inspect the *salitrera* early each morning. And I had shined his shoes in Victoria when I was nine years old, so he recognized me when I first came as an employee and so after some weeks I asked him for a favor. We were waking up at four, five in the morning to start in the dark cutting through the bones—" strange, Julio has a slip of the tongue and says first that they were cutting the bones of the people ... which is probably at least metaphorically true, then corrects himself and says it was, of course, the bones of the cattle that were being severed—"and it was dangerous, so I asked if the company could make us an electric buzz saw for the carcasses."

The result was that Alberto Bustamante Camacho—and I am impressed, not for the first and not for the last time, with how many names roll off Julio's tongue, the thousands of people he knew and remembers personally—Alberto, the head of *elaboración,* had a small engine tied to a rubber belt and a cutting tool made out of small sharp shovels being used in the rubbleworks.

And given the success of that venture, Julio Valdivia had launched yet another undertaking. He was worried about the lack of toilets. A matter of respect that employees of the company store should be shown, but bolstered as well by economic reasons—"one of the ladies working here would ask me if she could go and do her thing, which meant she'd be away for at least an hour at a time because she had to wander off into the pampa far from prying eyes," and so he'd persuaded management to build two *casetas,* one for men, the other for women.

It is this spirit, this ingenuity, this drive, of Julio Valdivia's that is so encouraging as well as endearing, the same incentive back then to do things right that he is now applying to the recovery of the *salitreras*. He is indignant—and Senén agrees and they stoke each other's anger as we continue to witness all that needs to be done, all that is waiting for a reprieve from decay—at how the other *pampinos* in the corporación, co-owners, after all, of this property, have not taken on the responsibility of raising the funds, do not volunteer for restoration work. "Sergio Bitar has done his bit," Julio complains, "but we can't keep on depending on someone influential to intervene and solve our problems. We're the ones who have to find a way."

I have been trying to figure out where Julio Valdivia's impulse comes from, where his ambition was born, how he managed to keep his illusions alive during a lifetime of frustrations and defeat. At his home yesterday in Iquique, in a tiny office space on the second floor of his unassuming house there, I had asked him to describe his first memory—hoping perhaps that I would be able to zero in on the one image he cannot rid himself of, the one thing he bequeathed to his future self as a young child, building his identity as all of us do, from the core of something wonderful he wished to repeat or something traumatic he wished to overcome.

And Julio Valdivia had recounted an incident—he was three years old so it must have been 1930, when so many of the oficinas were shutting down and the father of his dad had lost his job. "They'd closed Oficina Anita near Antofagasta," Julio said, his eyes narrowing, tightened to less than a slit, as he tried to recapture that moment, "and both my grandparents came to settle with us. The old man knew how to cultivate the land— so he started to plant cabbage, vegetables, and then would go to sell his produce in Pampa Unión. It should have been a joyous moment, my grandparents coming to see me, but he was so sad, my grandpa, and I loved him so much."

So his first memory was rooted in bereavement, someone in his family grieving for a home that was taken away. And Julio Valdivia would, like the viejos of Pedro de Valdivia, like

Hernán Rivera Letelier, like the parents of so many miners at Chuqui, spend the rest of his life watching other *salitreras* close, one after the other, until there was no nitrate town left to migrate to. What had been particularly painful were the final days of Victoria, where Julio had found work after Santa Laura and Humberstone had shut down in 1960. The distress he would normally have felt at having to lose his job and his house had been increased by a betrayal carried out by none other than ... General Pinochet. Who else would have promised thousands of workers in the theater of Victoria that he would never allow Victoria to be closed, that it would be the center from which the Pampa del Tamarugal would be reforested with the tamarugos that had once grown there, who else would have guaranteed that those who had retired from employment would be authorized to stay as long as they wanted, who else would have left the inhabitants to receive, the very next day, the news that they had forty-eight hours to abandon that town before they were forcibly evicted. "And I had totally believed that story," Julio had explained. "You know what my mistake was? Not to have left months before, gone to the highway outside Victoria and started a business buying the stuff being stolen from the town—if you saw how many people became rich by peddling the materials from that oficina and all the others."

I was taken aback at this revelation. Weren't his present enemies precisely the looters and merchants who would like to dismount Santa Laura and Humberstone? If he had participated in that despoilment back then, wouldn't he have been wrecking the very towns he now wanted to preserve?

"If everybody else was stealing, why not me?" came his answer. "No, no. We got the worst deal: We didn't stay and we didn't steal." Everybody who had worked in the *salitreras* had tried to take advantage of one last opportunity to make some money out of the dismantling process, called *desguace*. What had been built in a feverish race to create instant towns and extract as much nitrate as possible had then been disassembled painstakingly. Especially valuable was the *pino de oregón,* the pine from Oregon that was brought in by the ships that would leave with their holds overflowing with nitrate, but iron had also been much in demand, mostly during the shortages occasioned by the Second World War. And the tin roofs and the copper pipes and the faucets and the cobblestones and ... anything and everything that could be carried away had been subject to the depredations of the traffickers, paying desperate people a fee to raze the very houses they had lived in, demolish the streets where they had been born.

The fate of the sons of the salitre.

But now Julio Valdivia, toward the end of a life full of closings, is dedicated to the mission of opening, not one, but two nitrate towns. He and Senén and the others are attempting to reverse the history of Chile or, at the very least, to stem the tide of decay and save one territory of memory in the desert so future generations can understand the epic deeds carried out in this Norte Grande.

A bit over a week ago, in María Elena, Jorge Araya had shown me the long process of production that is required in order to turn the crust of caliche into white crystals of nitrate, I had watched hundreds of workers and dozens of trucks and smoke and movement and life. Here in Santa Laura all is quiet, the only sound in the stillness comes from the throat of Senén Durán as he steers me through the planta industrial that ceased to operate one morning forty years ago.

The machines are still here, inside this battered wooden structure as tall and as long as a small roller coaster, the *Chancho* where the first crushing occurs and the conveyor belt that used to take the material to the secondary grind of the *Chanchas*— using the male and female names of a pig for those jaws that pulverize the dry pulp into powder and send it on yet another belt to the *cachuchos,* large pools of iron that can hold up to six hundred tons of raw material. It is here that the Shanks system brought to Chile by Santiago Humberstone came into play, bringing the paste up to a boiling point through steam heat that circulates in tubes hidden to my prying eyes and my prying hands as I try to commune with the ruins of that machine that once had at its mercy the lives of all those men who have gone and never came back.

Senén Durán's stentorian, articulate drawl cuts off my thoughts: "As soon as the water reached boiling point—just as in so many recipes for cooking, right?—they stopped the heat from circulating and got the caliche out of these vats immediately. It had to be done quickly before the chloride could dissolve back into the mix—and then it was taken to those bins to crystallize, look, over there—" and we step outside the massive structure and into the sun again and approach the giant *bateas* that stand on wooden trestles where the nitrate would rest for a hundred hours. "It won't be the sun," Senén says, "it won't be the cold at night that will do the trick—just repose." And he pauses for dramatic effect and there is one of those angelic moments of absolute silence, which are much more absolute in the desert than anywhere else on Earth.

And I think of what the mineral has gone through—explosions, then being broken up, then carted off to machines that grind it into bits and then being scalded in water—and now a hundred hours of forced tranquility, like a wounded soldier recovering from battle. All to be able to continue its voyage, to return to an earth on the other side of the planet and nurture plants, make vegetables grow, renew that other earth with its Chilean salt.

And it is now that I learn something about Julio Valdivia that casts an unexpected light upon his existence.

"This was where I worked, what I did, when I was ten, twelve years old," he says. "Not here, in another *salitrera*"—he does not say where but perhaps it was Jazpampa where he was born and grew up—"I worked as a *rayador*." Senén explains that a *rayador de batea* had to scoop out the flakes left on the surface as the nitrate sank to the bottom of the trough, hours and hours smoothing out trough after trough with a stick called a *yegua*, a mare, yet one more farm name for an industrial activity. Mostly kids did this work, Senén says, just as youngsters were employed in so many other labors in the desert, the *destazador* with his hands small enough to reach in and widen the hole in the ground for the explosive, and the *lonchero*, who brought lunch to the men in the fields from their canteens, and the *cabero*, who would hook and unhook the wagons to the small locomotives that brought the caliche into the refinery.

I think of all those children working, Julio working under the hot sun for fourteen hours, and suddenly realize that over the last two days, not once had he mentioned this sort of menial job. At his home I had seen a photo of him, a nine-year-old shoeshine boy. But what he had done between that age and thirteen, when he began to work as an assistant baker in a *pulpería,* had been omitted. From the moment we had met he had presented himself to me as an employee, not a nitrate worker—that is the way he has construed the central narrative of his life, that is what gave significance to his existence as he lived it out, the fact that he escaped the fate of his forefathers.

That version of his identity—which does not include the backbreaking task of rayador de batea and who knows what other silenced toil that may have been even more perilous—starts with that photo snapped when he was nine, a mischievous look on an implike face and no shoes. Barefoot he might have been and almost penniless and yet was willing to spend what must have been a fortune at that young age to have his photo taken by a passing *fotógrafo ambulante,* already an indication that he thought of himself as worthy of another sort of destiny, had promised himself that he could be somebody else. That child of nine, in fact, would wait outside the canteen where the employees took their meals—"that's where the money was," Julio had told me yesterday at his home—so he could shine their shoes when they left, the clerks, the cashier, their shoes gleaming from his efforts. "The next day," Julio reminisced, "I would go to get paid and there was a *caballero* [a gentleman, a man of worth] sitting behind his own desk, and what was hammered into my mind, what I remember now, is that I told myself that someday I had to be like that man. That became my goal in life."

Santa Laura: Display of shoes worn by salitreros

It is that dream that fueled him all this time, that deeply explains why he is now going to move to Humberstone at the age of seventy-four. That dream kept in his sights as he worked in the troughs and rejected going on to the nitrate fields where most of his mates had ended up. Instead he had become an assistant to a baker in the *pulpería* at age thirteen—"I stoked the oven at three in the morning but was rewarded by being able to eat the bread bakers make only for themselves, the most fragrant meal in the world"—and must have proved himself adept because he then went on to be a *jornalero* (day laborer), selling coal and wine, and then was promoted to assistant butcher and from there became butcher and finally was given the job of assistant to the manager at the company store in Santa Laura and went on to be the second in command at the larger stores of Peña Chica and Humberstone and finally in 1962, two years after Humberstone closed, he found himself in Victoria as head of sales for the *pulpería*.

So what had he done when he arrived there? I had asked him yesterday.

"The first thing I did," came Julio's answer, "was to take a board, put a piece of green cloth on it, and top it with a windowpane, some glass on top, you know, and set it up on two trestles and there it was, my desk in the middle of the store."

It was an illusion of command that would last eighteen years. Until Victoria was also shut down and Julio Valdivia confronted the nomad fate that had hounded his grandfather and his family and everybody else tied to the nitrate cycle, the fate of the open road and homelessness that he had believed he could avoid.

Humberstone: Senén Durán and Julio Valdivia

And now, history has handed him the chance to prove that his life project was not a flickering deception. Humberstone is there, waiting for him—not a mere *pulpería* but a whole town to be administered. By rescuing Humberstone from ruin Julio Valdivia will also be rescuing his own dream as a nine-year-old shoeshine boy.

I am not making this up.

One of the first places that we visit as we walk along the streets of Humberstone is the house in which Julio Valdivia will settle a few days from now. We make our way to the room where he will install a new desk that looks out onto a nitrate town that, in a bizarre sense, will soon entirely belong to him.

There are four or five young workers who have almost finished their tasks—new floors, freshly painted walls, a sparkling clean bathroom and kitchen. Julio discusses with them the color of the paint, asks them what any homeowner might ask the men who are remodeling his home—don't the windows need a final wipe? what about this crack?—and then declares himself satisfied and turns to me. *This will be my bedroom, this will be where I'll cook, this where I'll place my desk.* His imagination brimming, not with a private past that I am shut off from, but with a future and public reality that will materialize as soon as these workers finish their job.

The crew comes from the South. Concepción, Temuco, again the people from a more fertile part of Chile being enticed northward by offers of work in a country that now, as then, has a high unemployment rate. They come to fix the places lived in so many years ago by men who had also migrated from the South in search of a better life. One of them, called Miguel, who is from Talcahuano, shows himself particularly interested in the history of that period. He feels half worker, half tourist, proud to be helping to save part of our history, part of his own history. I think to myself: Maybe he will stay in the desert, maybe he and his fellow workers will never return to the green of the South.

Miguel has something for Senén and Julio, a little gift. When the construction workers stripped from the windows the paper that had been protecting the room from outside dust and wind, they found, wedged there, a large yellowed piece of paper, drawings printed in Köln in 1924, with instructions in German on how to assemble the cachuchos, the water troughs—the same ones, I realize, where Julio worked during that forgotten part of his life, which he wished so desperately to escape and whose blueprints he will now triumphantly exhibit in the yet to be inaugurated museum of Humberstone, which Senén tells me will eventually be lodged in the Casa de Administración, the only structure left standing from the first days of this oficina when it opened in 1862 and was called La Palma by its Peruvian owners in remembrance of a battle outside Lima. Everything else was torn down and rebuilt when this oficina reopened in 1934, renamed Humberstone in honor of the old British chemist, who was still alive at the time.

We walk the streets of Humberstone and I am enchanted. No matter how abandoned those buildings may have been for the past decades, no matter that they are all shuttered up and crying out for the sort of repairs that Julio Valdivia's new house here has just received, this is still a place where you can easily imagine how life used to be like. This is what you expect from a real ghost town: everything run-down and yet intact, where you can almost feel the breath and presence of the people who once lived and loved here, where every corner calls to them to rise out of the past and start all over again.

It is what differentiates Humberstone from the one other ghost town I had already visited, a week ago on our way to Calama, the spooky Oficina Chacabuco, fifty miles from Antofagasta. True, the buildings of Chacabuco—which was inaugurated in 1924—are in a considerably sorrier state than those of Humberstone. Only the magnificent Teatro Municipal, partially restored with the help of a grant from the German government—can compare favorably with what I am now seeing in Humberstone. But the real contrast that Chacabuco offers is that it has not been entirely abandoned since it closed in 1940. Humberstone will, in fact, see a human inhabitant return for the first time in four decades when Julio Valdivia starts to sleep here this coming Sunday. Chacabuco has the sad privilege of having already been reopened—as a concentration camp for political prisoners after the 1973 coup. There is still barbed wire strapped to some of its walls, there are still signs posted warning visitors to be wary of the land mines that the military seeded all around the area to deter the captives from escaping. The Nazi-style watchtowers have been scrapped and the small houses where the prisoners were confined cannot, at first glance, be distinguished from the other structures in town that did not serve such dire purposes, but from the very moment you enter Chacabuco you cannot ignore its doubly tormented history, the suffering of the nitrate workers mingling with and overwhelmed by the more recent agony of the hundreds of men who were brought here from all over Chile to be punished for the sin of supporting a democratically elected government that did not want any citizen to ever again be treated in the way that the nitrate workers had been treated.

In the near future, when visitors come to Humberstone or Santa Laura, they will be greeted by someone who worked in the *salitreras* all his life, the Julio Valdivia who used to sleep in this very town. But when we had gone to Chacabuco the man who opened the gate for us was Roberto Saldívar, who had indeed slept in the place he was now supposed to guard in a quite different way: during the three months of his captivity that had followed his arrest and torture in Antofagasta in 1974. His mother, Estela, might have worked in Chacabuco when she was not even an adolescent, and he himself might have, out of curiosity, visited this former oficina several times as a young man, but it was not primarily the story of salitre that he wanted to keep burning and alive in the memory of whomever happened to pass through but the concentration camp experience—that was what had made him accept Sergio Bitar's offer to set up house in Chacabuco and become its guardian, what he kept returning to as he showed Angélica and me around. *Here was where we were interrogated as soon as we arrived. Here is where Waldo Suárez, Allende's undersecretary for education, the man who had visited Chacabuco in 1971 in order to see how a restoration could be funded, was stripped and humiliated by the soldiers. Here is where we had to rise every morning before dawn and stand at attention while the Comandante screamed at us. Here is where we used our time well, with classes of history, of foreign languages, of literature, imparted by the more intellectual prisoners.*

Without ever having stepped inside the boundaries of Chacabuco, I had often imagined life here, adding a shred of a story here and an anecdote there during my years of exile, as so many friends who had been jailed in that former oficina and then were released and banished told me about how they had survived the brutal weather and the even more brutal military detention. I knew how my pal Oscar Castro had staged plays for the captives and their jailers, and how the great folksinger Angel Parra had composed a cantata that is still played all around the world, and about the doctors who had set up a health clinic and the young militants who had started to write poetry and the small scalded tree that had been carved into the likeness of Christ by Orlando Valdés.

And there it was, that tree I had conjured up in my head during the nights of my banishment, there in the central plaza of Chacabuco, its branches stretching out like the arms of the crucified Jesus, its roots accusing the men who held the sculptor against his will—changing entirely my relationship and, I suppose, anybody else's to the gazebo it stands next to, not reminding us as the glorieta in Santa Laura does of the band that blared forth a waltz so someone like Julio Valdivia could dance.

The memories of the sorrow of those prisoners in Chacabuco clouding out the other memories, inhibiting the older ghosts of the nitrate past from making an appearance.

They are present in Humberstone, however, as Senén Durán explains during our walk through its streets.

"Remember," he says, "that this was meant to be a model town when it was built in 1934, incorporating all the rights workers had fought for over half a century. Laws for every worker in the land, not only for those who extracted nitrate. So this was the cradle of workers' rights and workers' organization for the whole country. In La Palma, right here, if we could go back to that time before it was remade as Humberstone, *no había escuela, hospital no había,* there was no school, no hospital, no temple, nothing, not a thing, no medical attention, no trade unions, no sporting clubs, nothing, *nada,* no Sunday rest, no vacations, no social security, no individual security, no electricity or water in each house, no Chilean money accepted, only tokens, nothing else."

"The administrators," Julio Valdivia interposes fervently, "felt they were gods and could do anything they wanted. In Humberstone workers were better off."

Even so, Senén takes me to see the *patio de los solteros,* a long dead-end street with rooms on either side, closed off by a padlocked gate, where single males lived under curfew. At the very end of the passageway are ten showers, ten toilets, ten sinks, ten of everything. Senén reads the set of regulations on the wall: forbidden to cook here, forbidden to keep food, forbidden to hold parties, forbidden to receive any visits in rooms, forbidden, forbidden, forbidden.

A more amiable face of Humberstone awaits us in the central square. Right next to the church is the first kindergarten of the Tarapacá region, organized by the Padres Oblatos, a Catholic order from Canada that had great influence in the pampa. And here is the *pulpería*—a lovely white building with an elegantly covered outside gallery—where Julio Valdivia worked till the last day in 1960 when this oficina closed down. It was, Julio says with pride, the most important company store in the whole Norte Grande because they had a refrigeration chamber, the only place in the desert that could store fish from Iquique before it was shipped by plane to Bolivia and Argentina.

I am then shown a series of shops that line two sides of the square, proof of an affluence that I would never have expected to find in any company town, that I certainly did not notice in María Elena during my recent visit. Senén explains and Julio reminisces and their voices blend into a low hum of memory piled on memory. Here was the bookshop of Armando Duarte, where the magazines and papers arrived before reaching Iquique or any other *poblado* in the vicinity. Just like the mail, first here, then other places. Because this was the hub and the pampa was more important economically than the coast. And here was the barbershop of Manuel Erisdaki, a Japanese barber—only for men, as women were attended at home if they had to do their hair. And here was where ice cream was sold—not in cones, but in cups, along with other desserts. And here was the seamstress who had all the latest fashions, "how I used to like to see the mannequins," Julio Valdivia murmurs. And look, here, Baldassano's hat shop. And the vegetable shop of Juan Chang, who never used a balance but weighed things with his hands and never ever was caught in a mistake.

And now the *Teatro*—the same four steps going up that we just saw in Santa Laura, but here they lead into a real theater, totally restored, where spectacles can be staged just as they were fifty years ago. "Though I'll tell you what," Julio confides, "I like the theater in Chacabuco more. That's where I saw my first movie, *El Día que me Quieras* with Carlos Gardel, the greatest singer of tango of all times."

But I hardly have time to digest this—the sun is starting to go down and there is still more to see, so off we go to an enclosed sports compound that has a large basketball court under the open sky. The posts at either end have recently fallen, curved over as if old age had brought them down.... By some miracle they have not yet been stolen by someone who could easily slip over one of the low walls that encircle Humberstone. While Senén and Julio note down that they need to find a way of buttressing up the posts or placing them in a secure place, I remember the story a friend of mine, Miguel Sayago, a prize-winning photographer, had told me about sneaking into Humberstone one night, after all the legal visitors had left. "If I don't see you go in," the guard at the door had said once he'd been slipped some money, "then you aren't here, are you?" Miguel swore he had found here, in the semidarkness, at the intersection of two forlorn streets, a young woman, naked, and crying. The proof of this was in a mysterious photo he had snapped and shown to me—though he has never wanted to disclose anything more about the incident, what happened to the woman, who she was, into what gloom she disappeared. I prefer not to tell Julio and Senén about this breach of security, and as to the naked woman—who knows how they would react to that?

And here we go again, down another street until we arrive at the door to the hotel of Humberstone and, once inside, past the bar where women were served Cinzano and past the billiard room, where the imprint of four legs can still be discerned. Julio Valdivia focuses on what seems to be his fondest recurring memory: the dance floor. We can see how the wood has been scraped and polished by thousands upon thousands of hours of shoes gliding along. Twenty-six years of tango and foxtrot and boleros. The orchestra at the back while Julio Valdivia and so many others whirled and twirled and sang along with the crooner. Julio's old face lights up with the memories of good times, glows whenever the subject of music is brought up. How they dressed up, he says, the *pampinos*— and I am reminded of the description given to me a few days ago by the poet Alberto Carrizo when we met in Iquique, the men who would descend on the city from the pampas, those workers who had cracked open rocks for the last six days baked by the sun and threatened with dust and wind and beatings from the foremen, and there they were in their smart black suit, red tie, white shirt, a watch hanging from a pocket, there they were, a black hat adjusted on their slick hair, some with shiny patent leather shoes, white socks, and an invariably white handkerchief. And each man, with three or four fountain pens ostentatiously peeking out of his jacket, brandishing his ability to write in a country where most workers were illiterate and silent. They would come, Alberto had said, to watch plays, to listen to music, mazurkas on the *pianola,* but also Mozart from the Filarmónica Obrera.

"And to dance," Julio Valdivia tells me when I mention this vision of Carrizo's to him, " we were always dancing, in Iquique and here."

At this moment, a group of schoolgirls—they must have descended from the tour bus that we saw parked in front of the entrance to Humberstone—burst into the dance hall, chattering and laughing. At first they are taken aback when they see us, three men talking in the gloom, but almost immediately one of them asks us if we know where the house of Mr. Flack is? Senén answers that they can find it in Pozo Almonte, that is where it's been taken. They look at him puzzled, as if he doesn't know what he's saying, then bid us good-bye.

"Mr. Flack?" I ask as their voices scatter into the distance.

It turns out that Mr. Flack is a character in a *telenovela,* a TV drama series called *Pampa Ilusión* that was filmed here in the year 2000 and that had been all the rage in Chile. A false vision of life in the *salitreras,* Senén snorts. More harm than good from that production.

At least, I suggest, some revenue must have come in that could be used to help in the preservation of Humberstone.

Not at all. When the TV company absconded, all they had left behind were two enormous containers of debris, a few spruced-up houses (where some cheerful curtains could still be seen hanging), and Mr. Flack's house—which the *pampinos* had asked the TV people to take away. After all, it was just a façade—deceitful as the promises the production company had made to contribute to the preservation of Humberstone. Like so many visitors to the pampa, these new TV callers had come, dug a hole, used up the resources, and then departed without helping.

The experience had left Julio and Senén angry and embittered. More people were coming to visit Humberstone, but they were not interested in the real history that had transpired here but in the fictional account that television had beamed into each Chilean home. Some come to this town to steal Oregon pine and others, the dream merchants, come to steal images and memories. Which made the plans of the corporación even more urgent. With not too much support expected from the government and not enough private charities willing to contribute, Julio Valdivia was pinning his hopes on a request to UNESCO to declare these *salitreras* a patrimony of humanity, reams of documentation that Sergio Bitar and he had traveled to Paris to present.

But for now they would have to depend on their own scant resources. And as if to prove that he means business, he points to a piece of wood that someone has unsuccessfully tried to jimmy away from the wall of the dance hall. He says to Senén that they need to come back with some workers and hammer it back into place. "Every day," he says, "every day, visitors steal something every day." And he closes the hotel's windows that somebody has left open....

We make our way through the gathering dusk to our last stop, what I cannot leave Humberstone without seeing: the enormous pool that was the delight of the *pampinos*. I had read somewhere that the pool had been built out of the empty hull of a ship that had been dragged across the desert and brought here to be filled with water. It pleased me to picture the iron husk of a ship meant to keep water out being subsequently used to keep water in. The image of someone pushing the gigantic shell of a steamer up the steep cliffs surrounding Iquique and then across the barren waste twinned the pampa in my mind with so many other Latin American enterprises madly penetrating Nature with objects of advanced civilization, perhaps best exemplified in the Herzog film where the crazed protagonist transports an opera house to the Amazon over mountains and through jungles. But alas, it was not true, according to Senén—the only maritime origin of the pool was the naval engineering techniques used to build it. Water was constantly being filtered and pumped up from a well that was forty-four meters down so the temperature was always relatively cool, a delicious bathing experience in that aggressive and dry environment. The pump and engine are still here, to one side of the stands where people would watch and cheer. "Then we'd go to the concession stand, *el bar lácteo,*" Julio Valdivia says, "where they sold *bidú* and *bilz*"—and I am abruptly engulfed in a wave of nostalgia for my own lost past, remembering these soft drinks, the colalike local beverages made in Chile itself that I had also guzzled upon my arrival in this country in the mid-fifties.

They fully intend to make this pool work again, to have the gardens bloom once more, to let the trees project "a green and fresh shadow" (Senén's words) as they had done in the past. They'll keep the old pump, as if in an open-air museum, and install two new smaller pumps to service the pool. Preservation, like everything in this desert, will juxtapose the old and the new, old machines and new technology.

"What about these trees?" I point to some majestic gnarled specimens of tamarugo.

"We'll uproot them, use them for firewood, replace them with new saplings."

I protest that they're beautiful, why not leave them?

"We want shade. We want everything to revive."

"And you don't feel sad at getting rid of these trees, which saw you bathe and play and drink?"

"No," comes Julio's reply, almost too quickly. "I want to see everything *verdecito,* green green. Have children playing on the grass."

Durán adds: "We have to say, Humberstone, *despierta.* Wake up. That's what we need to shout to this town."

This is not a bad place to end our tour, our day, as the moon comes up in a ripe, transparent sky.

It was right here that Julio Valdivia, then a vigorous thirty-three years of age, danced away the last night of Humberstone, next to the pool, on December 31, 1960, a boisterous farewell party attended by all those who were still left at the *salitrera* town. They danced until nine in the morning: the personnel at the *pulpería,* some security people, whoever else was around, some workers who had stayed on until they got paid. Nobody had been too drunk, according to Julio—not one of them had jumped in the pool, which was still full at that point. All very innocent, he says to me, that last night.

He is not inventing that innocence. The night watchman, who chanced by a few times that night, wrote in the log what he had seen: "I passed by the pool at four o'clock in the morning and they were dancing 'Mandandirún.'" They were dancing to a children's song, popular in Chile and in Latin America and Spain, something like "London Bridge" or "Here We Go Round the Mulberry Bush"—a song where half the dancers approach the other half and ask for their daughters or sons and take them off to be apprenticed as doctors, bakers, seamstresses, lawyers.

I think of it, try to conjure up the scene, those grown men and women of the pampa imagining some other destiny for themselves, nursery-rhyming themselves away from the shadows that were looming over their lives.

And because not one of them had wanted to say good-bye quite yet, because they all wished to prolong for a few hours more the illusion that Humberstone was alive, the whole gang had decided—once the sun had come up and started to broil away at them—to go off to the dance floor of the hotel where the party had only ended at one in the afternoon.

And what had Julio done then?

He had gone to the *pulpería*. All he had been doing the last few days was baking bread early in the morning, each day less and less as Humberstone shut down, as people abandoned the town, each day less of the bread he had learnt to bake when he was thirteen and had started out. But that day he had been dancing and had not baked any bread. So he simply went to the *pulpería* with his key and locked up the store where nothing remained, not even enough flour to make a loaf.

"Think of it," Julio Valdivia says, "there was a time when we used to receive thirty-two *quintales* of flour a day, and now there was nothing there at all."

"And then you left?"

"Yes," he says.

And smiles.

And I do not ask him if he had promised that one day he would return, I do not need to ask him if he kept the key.

Family Secrets

Friday, May 24, 2002. Iquique.

We are standing in front of a ledger, wide and thick and burdensome, with the dates 1885–1891 embossed on its dark
green surface, we are about to open this heavy book here in the
offices of the Registro Civil in Iquique, hoping that it contains
the answers to the questions about Angélica's lineage that we
have been fruitlessly chasing for the last five days.

Angélica and I did not want to end up here, in this building that houses the papers where births and deaths and marriages
have been recorded over the last 117 years, we have spent many
of our best hours in Iquique trying to avoid the sort of drudg-
ery that awaits us this morning, this sifting through endless
pages with their thousands upon thousands of surnames and
maiden names and given names in search of a few dry nuggets

of information. We wanted Angélica's remote past to be clarified by the thunderclap of a spectacular revelation, a story from
someone who personally knew the dead protagonists, a photo
that we could take home with us, a letter that unveils a truth
hidden by a century of evasions, a tombstone that silently
screams the one secret we are pursuing, the sort of lucky strike
that prospectors always dream of finding in the most sterile
waste of the desert, the vein that will lead to the mother lode.
Papers, documents, registers, books, the musty smell of
archives—none of this is romantic enough, none of it leaps out
at you with tales of betrayal, loss, enchantment by the sea, sex
and death and money. It is true that Iquique has offered us a
hint of this high drama as we combed the city for clues. This
was always going to be the place we would dedicate the most
time to, the real culmination of our journey, the one place
where the many spokes of our quest intersected. Here was
where Angélica's ancestors had arrived in search of fortune, here
was where the nitrate boom reached its apogee and transformed
a sleepy colonial town into a pulsing center of prosperity that
was a magnet for those immigrant ancestors, here was where
Freddy Taberna had lived and grown up and been arrested, here
is where most of the people we have been anxiously interrogat-
ing about one matter end up knowing something about the
others as well. And yet, after scouring cemeteries and meeting
several would-be relatives and knocking on doors of old mansions, after asking for help from lawyers who refused our
request for an interview and receiving that help from the
descendants of Croats whom we met entirely by accident, it
turns out that all of this feverish activity, rather than providing

us with the comfortable answers that we had been looking for, has instead opened up a series of disconcerting new questions. And that is why, on our last morning in Iquique, we have now reluctantly disembarked in this portentous hall full of women registering their babies and sad middle-aged men certifying the death of their mother and a lady who desperately needs proof of when her brother was born sixty years ago and these two sisters who need a copy of the birth certificate of their ailing father so a property can be sold before he expires and ... Everyone has their own little problem, their own puzzle to sort through, names that are spelled out to obliging young women who clatter away at computer terminals and hand out information and receipts and documents.

We are also looking for names and we know that they are not in those computers but buried, if we are lucky, in the ledger that we hold cautiously in our hands or perhaps in one of the many others that await our scrutiny, a plethora of possible names, brothers and daughters and spouses who could assist us in determining the story of the two men we are really looking for, one Malinarich and one Müller who came to Iquique from abroad sometime in the late nineteenth century and who never met as far as we can tell. It was their children who met sometime in 1915, one Malinarich son called Angel and one Müller daughter called Mercedes, who was a year older than Angel, that meeting in Iquique of two youngsters who were both in their teens so passionate and fruitful that on August 8, 1916, Humberto Malinarich Müller was born in Santiago. That baby boy who was to become Angélica's father and the father of her two sisters, Ana María and Nathalie, and her one brother, Iván

Patricio Frano, was not destined to be an only child. A year or so later, Mercedes Müller, Angélica's grandmother, was expecting again—and had hit upon what must have looked like a brilliant idea at the time: to ask her sister, Rosa, to travel from Iquique and help her out during her pregnancy and the subsequent delivery. Or maybe the suggestion had come from the husband, maybe Angel Malinarich had been looking forward to Rosa's visit with more anticipation than his wife; rumors circulate in the family that he had been Rosa's beau to begin with and that brunette Mercedes had stolen him away from the younger—and prettier—white-skinned and blond sister, perhaps Mercedes had got herself gravid with child in order to force a marriage that Angel did not really desire. We can speculate all we want about the dead—what is certain is that before the new baby was born, Angel Malinarich eloped to Argentina with his sister-in-law, Rosa Müller, probably sometime in 1917 or 1918. He died in Buenos Aires—again we have conflicting dates about when this event occurred—and never returned to Chile, though some twenty years later (at a date we are also trying to establish) Rosa crossed the cordillera back to Santiago, accompanied by a son, apparently named Rodolfo, a lad doomed to die of tuberculosis a few years later. As if that were not operatic and emotional enough, Mercedes had tearfully welcomed her sister back, declared her guiltless and blamed the wayward husband for the seduction.

Whoever would like to conclude from this noble gesture of reconciliation that Mercedes Müller had overcome the trauma she suffered from that double betrayal would be sadly mistaken. She had shown, it is true, exceptional dignity in dealing with the consequences of her ruin, refusing any aid from her husband's extremely wealthy family and going on to raise the two fatherless boys, Humberto and Mario, by herself, working for many decades as a secretary in the state railroad company. But it was also bitterness that kept her going, the masochistic satisfaction of feeling herself to be an eternal victim, a way of ensuring that her guilt-ridden sons would be forever in her debt, forever tied to her self-sacrifice and absolutely blind to the lengths to which she would go to destroy any woman who dared to come close to them. By the time I encountered grandmother Mercedes in the early sixties, she had already wrecked Humberto's marriage to Angélica's mother, Elba Saa, and was now intent on poisoning the love between Angélica and her father. It was only gradually that we realized that this was not sheer malice on her part, but that the old woman—she wasn't, in fact, that old, but looked gray and shuffled her feet wearily and hunched her back in order to inspire pity—happened to be verging on schizophrenia, a condition that increased as the years passed, as she became ever more deranged and perverse.

If Angélica and I now find ourselves about to inspect these ledgers in Iquique that may contain the keys to her genealogy, it is because her crazed grandmother Mercedes ended up being supremely successful in estranging Angélica from her father and his ancestry. At some juncture in my wife's existence—that coincided with the moment when our own relationship started to become serious and she was welcomed into my own very loving family—Angélica had decided that the only way to survive psychologically was to disavow that part of her past and pretend that the links to it did not interest her at all.

That may have been one of the reasons why we had never journeyed to the Norte Grande, even if Angélica kept stating that someday she really would have to visit Iquique. But every time a vacation was outlined, we always headed south to the woods and lakes or west to the wonderful waves of the Pacific or east to Argentina, where my parents were from and where—who knows—perhaps that lost grandparent, Angel Malinarich, was still alive, might welcome a visit. But no, Angélica had not wanted to contact him or even find out if he was alive. The last time anybody in the family had seen the philandering grandfather had been—according to Angélica's mother—when Humberto, already a well-known journalist, had looked his father up on a trip to Buenos Aires at some indistinct date in the early fifties. What was known about that encounter was as cryptic as that father's disappearance from Chile forty years before: The older Malinarich looked very young and fit and a ringer for his son. He had, he said, not remarried or spawned other children, and Humberto had introduced him to some colleagues at his hotel as "a friend," *un amigo.* But there was one major particular of their conversation that had found its way into the family legend. At some point—I don't know why, but I always conjured up coffee and cigars, a dessert maybe, a munificent Argentine meal that father and son shared in their only meeting in that city where I had been born—Angel Malinarich had said to Humberto: "*Hijo,* my son, you should go to Iquique and reclaim the fortune I left behind. It is yours. All you have to do is show up."

Humberto's reaction, according to Angélica's mother, had been to reject this offer. Perhaps because he had not wanted, like his mother Mercedes, to owe anything but his genes to the man who had abandoned him as an infant; but also, I would conjecture, due to the origins of a fortune derived from the exploitation of the nitrate workers. Tainted money for someone like Humberto who, at the time, was still a member—so this must have been before the XXth Congress of the Soviet Union, when the genocidal crimes of Stalin had been denounced—of the very Chilean Communist Party that had been born in the North of the country precisely out of the struggle against the robber barons of the *salitreras*.

Angélica, of course, another forty years later, had no intention of demanding that sumptuous inheritance her father had repudiated—but it certainly piqued her curiosity, contributed a certain detective-like tension to our search. Had that money ever existed? And if so, who had kept it all these years?

In the twisting center of the family's surmises about that immense lost wealth was the father of Angel Malinarich, whose story, or a semblance of it, we had been able to piece together from the many versions that Mercedes had poured into the ears of any member of the family who could sympathize with her penurious condition—Angélica's mother, Angélica herself, Angélica's brother, Patricio, all before the definite break with her had occurred. As I myself had received all of this in fragments, I had decided, before driving north, to visit Julio Saa in Santiago, a second cousin of Angélica's who was able to offer me an orderly account of the origins and vicissitudes of the Malinarich estate because his own grandmother Anna had been the best friend of Mercedes during the everlasting winter of her relinquishment and knew all the details. How Angel's father, whose name may have been Frano and whose mother's unknown surname we hope to ferret out of one of the documents gathering dust in the archives of the Registro Civil, had come to Santiago at some moment in the 1890s, where he falls in love with Carmen Pinto Benavides, a scion of wealthy landowners. This ravishing, dark-eyed aristocratic beauty believes that the dashing stranger—nobody has been able to pinpoint his age, nor do we have a photo—is the heir to the nitrate fields, *estacas salitreras,* and the equally profitable *pulperías* belonging to the Malinariches of Iquique. A marriage quickly ensues. Only when Carmela, as she was known, reaches Iquique does she realize that Frano is no more than an employee of his two uncles, the real owners of the business, a poor man who must spend most of his time in the inferno of the nitrate towns tending to their affairs. At a date that we may be able to determine today if we find his birth certificate somewhere in this building in Iquique, Angel Malinarich Pinto is born. He will eventually lose his father to one of the two habitual sicknesses—silicosis or tuberculosis—that plague men working close to nitrate extraction, but not before Frano does indeed inherit the extraordinary assets of his deceased uncles (and we'd definitely like to find their death certificates in one of these ledgers). On his deathbed he tells Carmela—still young and brought up to spend lavishly—that he is leaving her so much money that she will not be able to dispose of it in a lifetime. "If I give it all to you," Julio Saa reports him as having said, "you'll go crazy. So you're getting 70 percent and the rest will be for the workers I've been living next to these last few years and whose existence of misery and exploitation I wish to alleviate in some way."

What the widow thought of her husband's largesse has not been recorded (or even if such a liberal act ever existed), but she does take enough wealth back to Santiago in the early 1900s to live with her little boy in pomp and splendor, going off on shopping sprees to the department store Gath y Chaves and returning with two colossal cartloads of imported goods pulled by the packs of mules used for deliveries in those days. Carmela is imperious, with a temper of fire and a willfulness that knows no boundaries. She has many lovers and it is said that she consoles with the gift of a house each one that is dismissed. Meanwhile, Angel ends up as a boarder in the school of San Pedro Nolasco, from where, when he is fourteen, he escapes each night to go whoring and sneaks back at six each morning drunk and delirious, ready to pay the night watchman yet another hefty fee to let him slip out again that same evening. This is the boy who, at fifteen or so, goes off to visit the town where he was born, the Iquique that is at the source of all his wealth and where his path crosses that of the Müller sisters, the Iquique that we have just spent almost a week exploring, wondering in which of the corners of this marvelous city by the sea he first sighted Rosa or Mercedes and started on the adventure that would lead him to exile himself in Argentina, leaving behind an infant son who so many years later would, in his turn, give life to my Angélica.

And Carmela Pinto? When she realized that her daughter-in-law would not speak to her and that her son would never return, she took as many pesos and gold coins as she could fit into her handbag and followed her Angelito to the other side of the cordillera and spent the rest of her days, just like her son, in Buenos Aires, both of them dying a few years after that strange meeting between Humberto and his father in the 1950s in that Argentine hotel.

How much of this is true? And who were these uncles? And what is the real name of Angel's father? And where did he come from originally? And what happened to the money, if it ever existed?

That is what we have been trying to find out since we arrived in Iquique five days ago, late on the Sunday night of May 19.

We were welcomed by an auspicious sign. The first thing Angélica had done in the city that had not seen a member of her branch of the Malinariches return in ninety years was to throw open the windows of our hotel room and look out onto the plaza where her forefathers and foremothers had once strolled under the watchful shadow of the nearby white cliffs; Angélica had taken a deep breath and at that very moment, her watch had stopped. A statistical coincidence, of course. The battery was bound to run out at some point in time, but we humans discern patterns in random events, that is what has allowed us to survive as a species and to create art and religion and perhaps even science. So Angélica and I gave to that incident the meaning we desired: Weren't we, after all, hoping time would stand still, that the men and women who had made Angélica and whose blood coursed through the veins of our children and granddaughter would be frozen in a past that had not melted, waiting for our visit, waiting for her to come back?

Iquique: Plaza Arturo Prat

Fortunately we disposed of some leads that were a tad more tangible. One possible contact, Doña Carmen Malinarich Calderón, is the mother of a student attending the same university in Santiago as our niece Matilde—but there is only an answering machine on the other side of the line and we never get a call back. The other link proved to be more productive, even though we were greeted at first with suspicion by Vinko Malinarich, a thirty-five-year-old real estate broker whose father,

Antonio, had left his native Iquique for Santiago some sixty years ago. Again nitrate, always nitrate, determining people's lives—the fury of the boom enticing people to come, the fury of the bust chasing them away. Of the seven children of Antonio, Vinko was the only one who, at age twenty, had returned to his father's birthplace, where his family had apparently made their money in the Oficina Brac, later to be called Victoria—the very town whose closing had so altered Julio Valdivia's destiny.

Not that I was going to bring up the story of Julio Valdivia. Vinko was already wary enough about my call. His mistrust had slowly faded only when he heard that we had obtained his private number—and his cell phone as well—from a sister in Santiago. Angélica's brother, Patricio, the administrative director at the Hospital del Tórax, had given Vinko's father special attention when he was admitted for treatment and had proved even more helpful during the old man's last months of life. So Vinko, wanting to show his gratefulness, told us he would pass by our hotel three days hence, on Wednesday at noon, to drive us to his residence for an intimate family lunch. Before hanging up, he added that, though he knew very little about the past, there was a distant second cousin of his, coincidentally also called Vinko Malinarich, the principal at a school for disabled children, who was an expert in the family history and had scribbled out a detailed and comprehensive genealogical tree going way, way back and that maybe this other Vinko would be willing to show us the results of his exhaustive inquiries into the past.

Excited at the prospect of all that information awaiting our avid eyes, someone else having done our work for us,

Angélica and I debated whether we should not contact this second Vinko on our own instead of waiting almost three days, but thought it best to wait—which turned out to be a smart move.

Because meanwhile, what did we descry the next morning, Monday, May 20, on the exact other side of the exuberantly open plaza of Iquique but the Club Croata, a combination social club and restaurant run by descendants of the Croat migrants who, in the thousands, had come to the Norte Grande during the nitrate boom fleeing the Austro-Hungarian Empire that held their fatherland in its unrelenting grip and conscripted young males into a military service that they wished to escape. What better place for them than the rich pampas of Chile?

We lunched there that Monday the 20th, on our first day in Iquique, seated out on the plaza under a delightful sky and with a sea breeze rolling in from the nearby beach. And Angélica was able to acquire a fat, glossy volume entitled *The Croats, Nitrate and Tarapacá,* a five-year study of every minute aspect of Croatian life in Iquique and the *salitreras*. Its author, Vjera Zlatar, had even traveled to the Dalmatian coast in the former Yugoslavia to investigate the origins of all those men who, like the Malinariches, had crossed half the world to work and prosper and die in the desert of the Norte Grande. Professor Zlatar had carried out our research for us—she'd rummaged in the cemeteries, waded through the reports of the volunteer fire brigades and social clubs, ransacked hundreds of letters and diaries, read every newspaper of the era. There had to be traces of the family history concealed in those three hundred pages!

Angélica had been especially enthusiastic at the possibility of dipping into a Croat past that she had ignored for most of her existence. But over the next few days, Angélica had found in that Zlatar book a trail of clues that hinted at the existence of the elusive father of Angel Malinarich Pinto and his erstwhile uncles. Most impressive was the reproduction of an advertisement from 1908 offering imported olive oil and Croatian champagne sold at a store owned by the Malinarich Hermanos, the Brothers Malinarich. And later on, the same book mentioned two brothers, Frano and Pasko, who had been born in Kraljevica and by 1873 or 1874 were already installed in Iquique and owned a general store there, plus a *salitrera*. Maybe these childless brothers brought a Malinarich nephew from Croatia to help them, maybe he was the one who had wedded Carmela Pinto?

Yet, there are no photos, no names, not a whisper about the man we suppose was Angélica's great-grandfather.

There was a way, however, to settle all this, we were told at lunch the next day, Tuesday, May 21, by Sergio González, a sociologist who has written several splendid books on everyday life in the *pampa salitrera*. The cemeteries, Sergio announced to us, that was where the information lay, quite literally, at our fingertips. As he would have to leave for Santiago that very evening, what if he took us up the hill to the most beautiful graveyard in Iquique, the first and oldest one established in the city and where he did not doubt we could track down names and dates and connections. And we might also be able to do some research on the Müllers, the family of Mercedes that had also been on our minds.

Angélica assented to this proposal of Sergio's with pleasure. There was only one member of the Müller clan that she had kept seeing after the breach with her grandmother: Laura Müller, Mercedes's niece, and a prominent lawyer (with a stint as a justice on the Iquique Court of Appeals), had given Angélica refuge in her apartment in Santiago during the turbulent days of Humberto and Elba's divorce. While in exile, we had heard that Laura's only son, Fernando, an Allende supporter, had been murdered two years after the 1973 coup and that his heartbroken mother had returned to her native Iquique to live out the last years of her life. Laura was, in contrast to the slippery Frano Malinarich, a well-known figure to all Iquiqueños. Lautaro Núñez had, in San Pedro de Atacama, talked enthusiastically about the Müller household and given us detailed instructions on how to find it—and just about everybody else we approached had kind words for her. Though nobody seemed to know when Angélica's Tía Laura had died or where she was buried. So the visit to the Cementerio Número Uno of Iquique promised to unravel the tangled thread of the Malinarich lineage as well as allow Angélica to deposit flowers on the tomb of her Aunt Laura.

We did not make it to the cemetery that day.

On our way there, as we headed up the slope that is omnipresent in every port in the Norte Grande, every city on the coast hemmed in by mountains whose suffocating presence makes the majestic openness of the sea even more welcome, Sergio González suggested we stop the car. This was the house, he announced, of a friend of his, Ivor Ostoijic, an engineer who used the considerable money he had made manufacturing

Iquique: Angélica sitting on Tía Laura's chair

equipment to finance efforts to understand the nitrate past, particularly the role of Croats, subsidizing, in fact, the Vlatar book that had offered us so many insights into the lives of the Malinarich tribe. If he and his wife, Mariana, happened to be in ...

They received us as if we were long-lost brothers. Jolly and portly, their large bodies welcoming us into a spacious living room area absolutely brimming with books—our sort of people. But we couldn't stay very long; we explained we were on our way to see if we could find Laura Müller.

"Laurita Müller?"

Angélica ventured that she was a Müller herself, a relative of Laura's.

"Sit down in that chair, then," Ivor said, gesturing toward one of a set of extremely elegant chairs in the adjoining dining room.

Angélica was puzzled but did as she was told.

She was sitting, Ivor then told her, on her Aunt Laura's very own chair. His mother had bought the chairs and the dining table as a gift for them when Laura died some years ago.

Needless to say, we had stayed on at Ivor and Mariana's house for a few more hours, talking about Dalmatia and life in the *salitreras* and the murder of Freddy Taberna, whom they had known quite well, and when we rose to leave—invited back Wednesday night for dinner, who could refuse to sit in those chairs where Laura and her friends had lounged and chatted for hours!—it was much too late to visit the cemetery. But that did not really matter. This was how the quest in Iquique would go, we were sure, magically arranging encounters we had not expected, allowing us to find our way in a city that seemed to greet us at every corner, where everything seemed to connect.

Maybe this was a sign that our pursuit of the story of the Müllers would also begin to pay off.

The saga of that side of Angélica's family was both more grandiose and, if possible, more mysterious, than the Malinarich family line.

When I had first begun dating my future wife in the early sixties, one of the most intriguing stories about her ancestry dealt with someone referred to rather jocosely as *el pirata,* though he had not been a pirate at all. This Müller—at one point he was the father of Mercedes, in other versions, he was her grandfather—arrived in Peru sometime during the middle to the second half of the nineteenth century, bringing along, it was said, a shipload of Chinese slaves. Inverosimile, I had thought to myself. Slavery, after all, had been abolished by then and how had he passed through China, anyway, given that Mercedes insisted that he came, in spite of his Germanic name, from the Mediterranean. He had, she said, fled to South America from Greece, where he was both the physician of the royal family and the lover of the queen and had saved himself after a palace coup by dressing up in woman's attire, supplied, apparently, by Her grateful Majesty. (If there was any truth to this dubious story, then the year of that escapade would inevitably have been 1843, when the Greeks had revolted against a monarchy dominated by Bavarian influence.) This man, again according to the family legend, had proceeded to make a fortune for himself in Peru, probably in the *guaneras* (where the Chinese indentured laborers worked) or maybe the sugar plantations, a fortune that had been lost when the *montoneras* had swept his hacienda and stolen his buried treasure. Or maybe he had buried it and then forgotten where the booty had been hidden. What matters is that these bandits/guerrillas roved Peru during the lawless period that followed the total defeat in 1884 of the Peruvian Army by the Chileans in the *Guerra del Pacífico*. At some point this Müller—or then, again, it might have been his son—married a woman called Manuela Bustamante, whose family was among the most patrician in Peru, vaunting presidents and independence heroes and, of course, large landowners. Out of this union came several children over several decades, all of them born in Peru, the youngest being Mercedes Müller Bustamante and her sister, Rosa. At some point at the start of the twentieth century, the eldest brother, Demetrio, had moved the family to Iquique. Angélica remembered Demetrio Müller on his only visit to Santiago in the 1950s as a complete caballero, immaculately dressed in a dark suit and complaining that the traffic in this devilish capital showed no deference to him, one of Iquique's most prestigious citizens, did not even stop when he decided to cross the street.

Nor was the story of the Müllers entirely devoid of the sort of Sturm und Drang that afflicted the Malinarich clan. A certain Julia Müller, a champion swimmer who had been perhaps a niece of Mercedes, perhaps a cousin, one dawn went down to the sea and calmly disappeared into the surf and waves, preferring to kill herself rather than live without the young man she loved and who had been banished from the house by her parents. A story that seems to be substantiated by just about everyone we have been speaking to in Iquique, who keep some sort of memory of Julia's tragic demise, something their aunts or mothers or grandfathers gossiped about, that lovely young body washing up on the shore, the waste of it all.

Though our ever ready informant Lautaro Núñez had also vaguely recalled something about a Julia and her lover and a drowning, other knowledge he imparted had been notably more precise. He explained quite minutely how to reach and recognize the house that had belonged to the Müllers, the house where Angélica's grandfather had gone to ask for her grandmother's hand, and that might still hold some clues to what had become of the family. Everybody knows everybody in Iquique, he said.

True enough. The first night in town we had been visited by the architect Patricio Advis, one of Lautaro's friends, who had spent much of his existence trying to make sure that the city would not be swallowed up by the malignant gods of pollution and sprawl that accompany progress, and was therefore painfully aware of the many avenues of its past. If we wanted to find out everything about both branches of Angélica's family, he had just the person: a certain Mrs. Bolton, a decrepit old woman who lived on the same Baquedano Street where Don Demetrio had reigned supreme. Not that Advis was overly hopeful. *Nobody remembers, nobody cares,* he sighed. *That world is gone—with my father, with my mother.*

Not entirely gone. Baquedano Street has been lovingly preserved, house by Victorian house, and it was down that street that we took our first stroll in Iquique our first morning in the city where Angel Malinarich had brought his bride

Iquique: What is left of the Müller residence, now a high school

Carmela Pinto over a century ago, we walked along Baquedano until it intersected five blocks later with Bulnes just as that great-grandfather must have done.

"This is it," I said to Angélica, and there it was, just as Lautaro had described it, the corner house two stories tall, where the Müllers had once lived. We were excited. It did not seem deserted, even if some windows were shuttered and others had the curtains drawn. We knocked on all three of its doors (on both streets, just as Lautaro had recalled them) and also tried rapping on the windows. Nobody answered. Half an hour later, on our way back from the seashore six blocks away, we stopped at a small shop right next to the Müller house. The girl selling ice cream and soft drinks behind the grocery counter was, like most people in Iquique, affable, and most ready to consult her ancient and hidden grandmother. This is it, I murmured to Angélica, we're about to strike it rich. But the voice we were soon able to hear from behind some curtains at the back of the store croaked out that the old woman who lived next door had died a mere month ago and that the house was closed while the family decided what to do with it. We had the sinking feeling that we'd just missed the last link to the past—could this be a remnant of the Müllers, our chance to find out if the Greek ancestor ever existed, if cousin Julia really did walk into the sea? And yet, after further consultation with the secluded granny, we were further informed that the name of the recently deceased neighbor was May Nichols—or that is what it sounded like—an Englishwoman who had lived there for the last ninety years.... No Müllers, we hear the grandmother say, not in that house. So far from having missed the boat, perhaps there was no boat to begin with, maybe Lautaro had been confused.

When we told Patricio Advis a few hours later about our little detective work, he was saddened. "Oh dear," he had said. "*Se nos murió la Tía Grace,* our Auntie Grace went and died on us."

He was talking about the very woman he had mentioned the previous night, the one survivor from the nitrate era who could have given us some intelligence regarding the past, the sister of Lily Bolton, whose married name was Grace Maine-Nichols. So Angélica and I, rather than detectives of the dead, have come as their messengers, delivering the sad news that Advis himself had not yet heard.

And Lautaro is mistaken, Patricio said. That house never belonged to the Müllers; it has been part of the Nichols family for the past hundred years. The Müllers live in another part of town—and he then drew us a map—"Look, you go along

Covadonga Street, and it's here." He was sure, as he had been quite close to Laura Müller, particularly in the years after the coup, when she had returned to Iquique. He had never thought to ask her anything about where the family came from—and anyway, people stopped speaking to each other during the dictatorship. Nobody knew anymore who was who. The identity of Iquique changed—people were scared of talking about themselves. They shut themselves up, he said, inside their own thoughts.

Patricio himself had seemed lost in thought, in musings. Laura, he said, was part of the landscape. Like the universe, like a star, he thought she would always be there. Like Tía Grace. *Y ahora se nos fue de Iquique.* And now she's left Iquique.

He remembered Laurita's father Demetrio just as Angélica described him: slender, his skin more on the dark side, very elegant, only using the finest English cashmere suits. And the servants all wore white gloves when they served dinner. Demetrio had made his money in the export/import business and had educated his children at the best schools and universities. Maybe he was the one who had helped his sister Mercedes when she had been forsaken by her husband, though Patricio knew nothing about this Angel Malinarich we were seeking.

That evening we cleared up the mystery of the ever shifting Müller house. Oscar Varela, Freddy Taberna's best friend in Iquique, told us, over another of those never-ending *onces-comidas,* that Demetrio had indeed originally lived on the corner of Baquedano and Bulnes—diagonally in front of the Maine-Nichols residence—but that the Müller mansion had been expropriated by the municipality many years ago to expand the Men's High School. The outlines of the old mansion could still be discerned under the new construction. Demetrio had moved to Covadonga after that—a house just down the street from Oscar's, where Laura died. The one who could have resolved all our doubts was Oscar Varela's mother, who had been so close to Laura, but his mother had died several years back, so … And that was how it had been, with Patricio and with Oscar and with Ivor and with el Pelao Gavilán, a kinesiologist who runs El Galpón, a marvelous restaurant in Iquique. Another of Lautaro's buddies, another friend of Freddy Taberna's, brimming with information about everything in the Norte Grande and full of recipes for the most inventive dishes, combining exquisite native dishes with the many cuisines from around the world that had flooded into this region, delicate meals he cooked for us four out of the five nights we had spent in Iquique, but unable, Gavilán, just like the others, to solve the riddles of Angélica's past. "That's how life is," Gavilán had said on Tuesday evening. "By the time you are old enough to want to find out about your genealogy, it's too late; the elders with the knowledge have all died."

And the one person we have tracked down who is old enough to remember everything about the Müller past, a ninety-year-old lawyer named Raúl Arancibia, who had been one of Laura's senior colleagues on the Iquique Court of Appeals, had refused our requests for an interview—perhaps because, as a Pinochetista, he wants nothing to do with Allendista scum like me.

So our hopes turned back to the Malinarich gang, to our upcoming lunch with cousin Vinko, the real estate broker. When he walked through the door of our hotel on Wednesday,

May 22, I immediately noted his family air, a certain resemblance to Angélica's brother, Patricio, but Angélica is not that sure—though there is one unmistakable Malinarich trait, a high forehead with slightly receding hair on either side of the scalp, and that is already a living lesson about how the past persists, even if Vinko himself, as he had already confessed over the phone, was almost entirely ignorant about the family history. In the course of the seafood meal he treated us to near the very docks where his forefathers and Angélica's had disembarked over a century ago, he grew ever more animated and friendly. Maybe he had realized that we really were legitimate relatives with no ulterior motives in tracking him down. Had he been worried that we were coming to reclaim the lost fortune? Was there even a lost fortune to be worried about? He did not broach the subject and we did not bring it up.

Later on, Vinko took us on a Malinarich tour of the city, in other words, a vision of Iquique overflowing with descendants of the four Malinarich brothers who emigrated here at the end of the nineteenth century from the Dalmatian coast, none of them even closely related to the Angel Malinarich we were seeking. It was hard to keep track of them all. The orthopedic shop of Carmen Malinarich stood out (a different Carmen than the one who had not answered our phone messages) and Larry Malinarich, an artist who had painted a mural in the Club Croata, and Yerko Malinarich, a captain in the police force, and, above all, the other Vinko Malinarich, the self-proclaimed expert on the family genealogy, at whose school this first Vinko ended up depositing us, before rushing off in his Jeep to secure a sale on a commercial piece of property.

Vinko the professor had looked harried—who wouldn't?—at our poorly timed appearance. Was this because these distant so-called cousins erupted into his office without warning precisely when he was trying to resolve several crises regarding the disabled or retarded children who studied at his school? Or was there a deeper mistrust in his eyes? At any rate, he suggested that we assemble at our hotel tomorrow, say at eleven, when he would show us all the pertinent documents.

Tomorrow was Thursday, May 23, and our time in Iquique was running out, but who else was offering us a genealogical map of the family and who knows what other goodies, so the next day found us waiting for him. Eleven o'clock and nothing. 11:15. 11:20. What if he had decided not to make an appearance, had never intended to come at all? Could it be that his father or grandfather or somebody in his family had bilked Angel Malinarich Pinto out of his money a century ago and this Vinko and his siblings—wasn't the Carmen who had not answered our urgent phone messages the sister of this Vinko?—had been warned that a day would come when strangers from Santiago bearing their same name would come to reclaim their inheritance?

Our imagination was working overtime. At 11:25, schoolteacher Vinko, with his typical Malinarich forehead and a benign smile, made his loyal and apologetic appearance in the hotel lobby and proceeded to pull from his briefcase a sheaf of papers. First of all, three long foolscap pages filled with more Malinariches, many generations of them, than we could ever have absorbed in several sittings, sons and daughters and wives and brothers, all descended from four brothers, Frano and

Anton and Mateo and Milen, who had, apparently, come to Iquique in 1890. And family photos and a copy of a passport from 1893 from the Austro-Hungarian Empire.

The attitude of our newfound relative was a curious mixture of amiability and evasiveness. He copiously shared with us all that he knew and had made facsimiles of his documents and seemed sincerely interested in our own rather skimpy and incomplete family tree. And yet something did not quite fit. When I pointed out that certain dates for his family's arrival in Iquique could not be reconciled with evidence available in the book about the Croats that Angélica had been assiduously poring over, he was dismissive, both of the book itself and of the Croat community in general, insisting that his family had refused to be interviewed for that volume, that they preferred to be anonymous, not mix with the offspring of those other immigrants. Even so, he had been exceedingly affable all through our conversation, peppering it with a slew of anecdotes from his side of the family, explaining how difficult it was to get funding for special education these days, and, at the end, suggesting that, in the future, we stay in touch and exchange information.

Once he was gone, I had looked at Angélica and then at my watch. This was our last afternoon in Iquique and I needed to head for Santa Laura and Humberstone with Julio Valdivia and Senén Durán in two hours' time, but if we hurried we could rush up to the cemetery. Maybe the graves could tell us something that the living, thus far, had been unable or unwilling to disclose.

We did, indeed, find Laura Müller's tomb—a small niche that at least contains one tiny piece of information we had been seeking, 1981, the year of her death. But there was no sign of any other family member—not her father Demetrio Müller Bustamante, not any of his brothers or sisters, not a whisper of the suicidal Julia, and certainly no trace of the still unnamed grandfather who had presumably come first to Peru and then to Chile.

So we snapped our pictures and wandered farther afield, attesting to the multiple nationalities and languages that had swamped Iquique during the nitrate cycle, the whole history of the Norte Grande concentrated in this one space, the ultimate ghost town of them all. The influence of desert-life everywhere. The older graves still adorned with flowers made out of paper or of tinsel burnished in many colors, a way of honoring the dead in a place lacking water or fresh flowers. And the streets that ran north to south taking the names of Oficinas Salitreras—Brac, for instance, or Esmeralda, or Alemania—and those that went east to west, the names of the ports from which that nitrate had been sent off, *caletas* such as Pisagua or Junín, so that here too, the sea and the pampa meet, intersect in death as they did in life, still fighting for supremacy so many decades later.

And then some Malinarich headstones—Familia Malinarich Alecchi on the Salitrera Buen Retiro and Guillermo Malinarich (1886–1962) smack in the middle of Caleta Buena and none of them, not one inscription, not one murmur of a stone engraving, divulging the names or remains we were looking for. Haunting and significant and sobering but also silent, this Cementerio Número Uno, the oldest one in Iquique.

And that is why now, on our last morning, this Friday, we are leafing through this musty ledger that contains no more than the handwritten names of those who were born in Iquique from 1885 onward, desperate to find something, anything, that will reward our pilgrimage. In that first burdensome tome, we unearth two babies, Ernestina Malinarich Gonzalez, born in 1888, and Georgina Luisa Müller Díaz, born in 1889—and in subsequent volumes, more and more Malinariches and Müllers come into the world but nothing that we don't know, here are all the children who eventually filled the cemetery we have just visited yesterday, we already know where their journey ends, the tombs that have nothing to tell us, the register that also seems to be mocking us.

Even so, the dusty archives begin to yield, as if they were pieces of caliche we were grinding out, tidbits of information, some of which confirms the stories grandmother Mercedes used to tell: the birth certificate of cousin Julia, the one who walked into the sea; the Peruvian origins of the Müllers; the fact that Mercedes and Angel were indeed adolescents when they met, when Rosa watched her sister steal away the man she loved.

But as the Registro Civil closes—and we cannot come back, we have promises to keep, the Pisagua where Freddy Taberna was murdered awaits us this very evening farther north—it dawns on us that we are leaving Iquique without having clarified any of the mysteries we brought with us. No memories of the first Müller who crossed a turbulent sea, no tomb or death certificate of the great-grandfather of the Malinariches who presumably died of too much exposure to the desert and dispensed a lost fortune to his heirs. These men, whose name Angélica carries, whose blood runs in the veins of my children, have disappeared from the face of the Earth as if they had never existed. A fate worse than the ruins of the saddest *salitrera*.

And yet, we feel almost giddy as we retreat from Iquique, mount the steep cliff, say good-bye to the bustling streets below, pass by the dragon hill that guards this port, the hill children are still rolling down as they must have done in the time when Angélica's forefathers and foremothers inhabited this strip of land by the splendid sea.

We depart energized. Much of what has been reiterated for generations in the family lore has been proved accurate and we may, therefore, in the future, use those tidbits preserved by an oral tradition—to continue our search. Santiago awaits: where the death certificates of Mercedes and Rosa may yet hold a surprise or two and where other Müllers could well have kept some memory, some letter alive. And Buenos Aires awaits: Perhaps we can track down someone who knew old Angel Malinarich, perhaps Carmela Pinto, so extravagant in her youth, left behind some flaming reminder of her presence in that city. And Kraljevica awaits: The next time I am invited to the opening of a play in Croatia, rather than demur as I have in the past, I will accept and use the opportunity for Angélica and me to visit the town on the Adriatic that once saw all those Malinarich brothers and cousins and nephews and uncles leave for America and that must have records of relationships, baptisms, deaths.

But what awaits us above all is Iquique.

We have fallen in love with this city that also must have seduced Angélica's ancestors. Both my wife and I have been irritated with Chile for the past decade—meaning Santiago, with its smog and envious elites and stunted democratic reforms and persistent amnesia and petty grandiloquence. Santiago forces us to remember in every gray corner of its congested and hurried streets what we had once dreamt our country could become, a dull intimation of how time and history have denied those dreams. Iquique is an open, generous city, that has given us a fantastic welcome, where we leave new friends and standing invitations to come back, and Angélica in particular has felt a warmth here that has been lacking in so many of our other returns from exile. But there is more in this love affair with Iquique than the friendliness of its inhabitants or the pace of life or the heavenly beaches or the perfect temperature. Some bitter abyss that separates Angélica from her past has been breached, the barrier that kept her from exploring and accepting her origins. It is this recognition of Iquique as a city that belongs to her as it had belonged to the men and women who made her that may be more significant than the names of this ancestor or the birthplace or burial ground of that one. The past will always be incomplete—it is even healthy that part of it should remain mysterious and distant, somehow fitting that ghost towns also be left to the ghosts rather than hunting down their every secret and pretending that we can entirely understand what is, after all, dead and gone. We are finally condemned to leave unlit many of the darkened patches of the history that forged us, leave behind us the debris of our own lives. But we owe it to those who came before and to those who will come afterward and sift through the legacy we bequeath to at least make the attempt.

The last time a Malinarich climbed this hill into the desert was ninety years ago when Angel Malinarich Pinto took his bride, Mercedes Müller Bustamante, on a trip through the desert to Santiago from which neither of them would return.

I am not sure if my darling Angélica Malinarich will ever come back, as she has promised, to Iquique, but I do know that she has, in more than one sense, come home.

Finding Freddy

Saturday, May 25, 2002. Pisagua.

I am standing in front of the cell where Freddy Taberna spent his last night on this Earth, I am here in this jail in Pisagua where my friend Freddy was informed by its military commander that the next day at dawn a firing squad was to execute him, I am remembering Freddy in this jail that has, so many years after his death, been converted into Pisagua's only hotel.

A hotel built on the premises of the old jail, a hotel where hundreds of political prisoners were incarcerated after the 1973 coup. The hotel where Angélica and I slept last night.

Pisagua had always resonated malevolently in my mind as a blighted place, a port cursed by history. Inhabited, as Arica had been, by Chango Indians for millennia before the

Spanish arrived and as prosperous as Iquique during the nitrate boom, visited by illustrious scientists like Darwin and by infamous buccaneers like Drake, it had not become a ghost town itself after the fall of the *salitreras* only because it had been able to market the one product it had with more abundance than any other place in an already godforsaken Norte Grande: its extreme, almost abject isolation. The government had built here in the late 1920s a small penitentiary whose thick walls were much less an impediment to prison breakouts than the abrupt surrounding cliffs and the expanse of desert beyond, so that the whole town could itself be considered a stockade, which meant that it could also be used as a convenient dumping ground for the politically suspect. This employment of the once flourishing port, which would culminate with the incarceration of thousands of Allende backers from 1973 onward, had begun timidly enough with a few dozen German and Nazi sympathizers confined there during the Second World War.

But in the late forties, at the start of the Cold War, things turned more serious when President Gabriel González Videla had ordered a concentration camp built for enormous contingents of communists. What made the latter episode particularly nasty was not only that the camp had been commanded by none other than Augusto Pinochet, then an army captain (training for his future role as dictator of Chile), but that González Videla was immuring in Pisagua the very men who had helped elect him and been a crucial part of his administration during its first years, in effect persecuting his own friends and allies. This was one of the many reasons why

Angélica had felt qualms about accompanying me on this part of the journey. Her own politically active father, Humberto, had avoided being sent to Pisagua only because he had managed, by a miracle, to flee when plainclothesmen came for him in the dead of night. Came for him even though González Videla was Humberto's godfather and had lived for free in the house of grandmother Carmela Pinto when he first arrived in Santiago to study law in 1916, the very year that Angélica's father had been born.

Angélica's distaste for this trip to Pisagua could also be traced to other, more immediate reasons. She had heard that the descent to that town along a steep escarpment was exceptionally dangerous—and there was nothing that my wife dreads more than curving and perilous roads. I convinced her that there was no cause for alarm even while I readied her for a rough ride. But I had not anticipated, nor seen previously on a trip already teeming with barren landscapes, vistas as scorched as these. Once we had lurched off the main highway that led from Iquique to Arica, there had been, for the next thirty miles, no sign of human habitation except the remote ruins of a village, far off to one side of the road overladen with potholes. A road? I am being magnanimous. An assemblage of gashes barely bound together by an attempt at pavement. And yet—consoling myself and Angélica with something, anything—a valuable experience: what other way to access how terrifying this desert can be if you wander off the main highway, how else to gain a faint intimation of how it must have appeared to the original explorers as they trudged toward Pisagua. And once we'd rattled our way through these dunes and grit, our windshield caked with dust and our vision made worse by a swiftly setting orange sun, down, down we started to go, sure that the car was going to fall apart, down, down, down into a frightening gorge that ushered us, not as we had hoped, to the sea, but to the top of an almost sheer cliff—and way down there, almost a precipice of a mile below, was an irresolute couple of streets with two rows of fifty or so houses clutching the shore, as if its residents did not know which was worse, the loathsome mountain or the savage sea. But that was our dubious haven and we had better get there quickly: Roaring in from the south and the ocean, we saw a rolling white bank of clouds falling onto the bay and the town, a thick dense curse of a fog crawling downward, a fogfall, if such a thing could be said to exist, falling like water, a fogslide submerging itself downward, like the dark paw of God, threatening to swallow the narrow, winding, zigzag road that had barely been hewn from the rocks, threatening to engulf us and our car before we even made it to the ambiguous sanctuary of the esplanade. That was our welcome to Pisagua: the fog that overran this simulacrum of a town five minutes after we had arrived, allowing us to scarcely note the strange beauty of this port of 150 souls, once the pride and joy of the nitrate industry, where opera companies from Milan came to play and Sarah Bernhardt declaimed Racine, this piece of land still dreaming of when its buildings were not derelict and British gentlemen escorted white-laced ladies with parasols under the magnificent tropical palms and immense gnarled trees that still line its seacoast today.

A far more dire greeting was in store for us.

After groping our way through the dismal haze and missing

Pisagua

Pisagua's lone hotel several times, we had finally managed to park the car in front of what seemed the façade of a splendid very tall two-story Victorian mansion flanked to its rear by a hulk of dank concrete that brought to mind the architecture of the ugliest public housing projects. There was not even a light on, not the faintest promise of human occupancy. I knocked on the enormous door while Angélica watched me reproachfully from the car. Nobody answered.

"Are you sure somebody's there?" Angélica called out. She had already warned me that she was not going back up that cliff in this fog and at dark.

I didn't answer. I couldn't be absolutely sure if anyone would greet us at all. I had been told that the hotel was often closed—not strange as at times weeks passed without anyone coming through—but our reservations had been made through Natalia Varela, the powerful head of tourism for the region of Tarapacá and another of Sergio Bitar's friends who had helped plan our stay in Iquique and who assured us that the owners had decided to open it up especially for us. But what if there had been some mistake, some confusion in the date, some last-minute problem? Maybe instead of sleeping in the prison where Freddy and his brother and Oscar Varela and so many others had been cast, we were going to have to camp out on the rocks, among the ruins. And who knew if that was not a better solution, a bit less ominous and morbid, a better homage to our murdered friend?

I knocked again.

Sounds from within. A dim light sputtered on inside the hall and the door yawned open. Standing there was a small tyke with a crewcut, who couldn't have been more than five or six years old. He looked up at me insolently, not saying a word.

"Is your mother around?"

The kid shouted, *"Mamaaaá,"* and a female voice had answered from inside the hotel, followed soon enough by a young, blondish, good-looking woman in her mid-twenties, who informed us that she had been expecting us and to come round to the side street and park our car where it would be safe.

Angélica had joined me by then and, trying to make believe that this was the most normal of visits and this the most ordinary of hotels, addressed to the child the question one always asks any kid to break the ice:

"*¿Y tú, cómo te llamas?*"

What's your name?

And the reply, before he disappeared into the cavernous maw of the hotel:

"Augusto."

We looked at each other with more trepidation than if he had said Dracula. Anybody in Chile who baptizes one of their offspring with the name of our former tyrant has to be a real fanatic, the sort of person we would rather avoid—and more so in this place, where almost thirty years ago one of our friends heard his death sentence pronounced by a military tribunal that was acting under the orders of the man whose name this child bears so proudly.

And so, penetrating in that hotel warily, as if the very shadows might attack us, we bolstered ourselves for what was going to undoubtedly be a dreadful evening.

Not at all. The hotel premises, lovingly restored, occupy the old administration building adjoining the penal colony and the rooms on the ground floor still keep many of the fixtures from the era when that building was first erected and furnished, the chamber where a judge presided, the office that served for the Registro Civil of Pisagua in better times, the recreation room for the guards and officials where little Augusto is entranced hour after hour by warlike cartoons. More charming is an inner patio with bougainvillea and semitropical plants and flowers, surrounded by a walkaround gallery, where we sip a much-needed pisco sour, while we take a gander at a jumble of mementos on display. Bottles from old pharmacies and locks of all sorts and desiccated crabs. Victrolas and extinct cameras and ruined typewriters and clocks—the hotel is full of ancient clocks, each one stopped at a different time of day. And some left-wing posters, of Neruda and Violeta Parra and Victor Jara, as if the decorators wanted guests to understand that they were not the ones responsible for whatever horrors might have occurred in the penitentiary that looms in the back. And dispersed everywhere: souvenirs from the *salitreras* like the ones I had seen in the Casa de Administración in Santa Laura, tokens, implements, photos, woolen socks that protected workers from the boiling waters of the vats. Our hostess was hospitable and seemed supremely naïve, claiming that this was not a bad way to make a living, in a place that she said was healthy for her child and where her husband—away, thank God, on business— can dive to his heart's content. She had served us an excellent and inexpensive dinner before leading us upstairs to our room along a staircase that reeked—I am not inventing this—with the smell of some dead animal, a rat decomposing under the floorboards, a corpse, a corpse, and I had suddenly panicked, flooded by the memories this place conceals; but the rest of the hotel is clean and quiet, except for the intermittent screeches of a white parrot hopping inside a gigantic birdcage nestled in the patio. And our bedroom, with its lofty walls and antique dresser and creaky bed, reminded Angélica of the room in the countryside where she dreamt away most of her childhood and a good part of her adolescence. So it was not long before she fell asleep, exhausted by a day that had started in the Registro Civil of Iquique and was followed by hours of desert crossings and a final descent into the inferno of Pisagua.

I had things to do before turning in for the night, before closing my eyes.

I went down to the sea—a few yards away—and concentrated on my yoga exercises, quietly breathing in and breathing out and trying, very deliberately, to focus on Freddy. His cell was right behind me, slightly above me in the nocturnal mist that hung on the trees, that dripped from the leaves of the trees. This is what he must have heard on his last night and if I was sure of anything it was that he had not slept at all, he would have been listening to these sounds, the waves and its tide of pebbles, the *pi-pi-pi* lament of seabirds, the barking drone of dogs, the entreaty of the wind. I sucked in the insanity of being here, that I was alive and he was dead, the juxtaposition and contrast of beauty and horror, of normality and aberrance, that dismays and amazes and intrigues me, how we could enjoy the dinner and at the same time feel tugging at the edges of our attention that nearby block of concrete that had housed so many desperate men during so many desperate hours.

How had Freddy ended up here, listening to this same sea during those last hours of his on this planet we had shared with such joy and hope?

I had been drawing closer to Freddy these last few weeks, retracing the steps that had brought him here, getting to know him much better in death than I had in life. Starting with a three-hour conversation with his widow, Jinny, in Santiago and continuing with the long reminiscences offered by Lautaro in

Iquique: Oscar Valera and his wife, Leyla, holding a photo of Freddy and Jinny when they lived in Iquique

San Pedro de Atacama and by Oscar Varela and his wife, Leyla, in Iquique and scraps of information gathered in almost every chance encounter, talking to Senator Ricardo Núñez and Ivor Ostoijic and Sergio Bitar and Senén Durán and Sergio González and Guillermo Ross-Murray Lay-Kim, everyone we had met seemed to have a Freddy Taberna story, the most crucial tale of all told to me in the midst of the clack of roulette tables at the casino of Iquique the night before Angélica and I had left Iquique, that night when I finally encountered Pichón Taberna, Freddy's half-brother, the last person to speak to Freddy before he died.

I had always known, from the moment Freddy and I met, that he was an exceptional human being, but it has only been now, as I journeyed from Santiago toward Pisagua in search of the place and circumstances of his execution, that a real picture of his saga has begun to emerge, even more extraordinary than I had suspected during our youthful years.

Freddy had been an illegitimate child, brought up mainly by his Peruvian grandmother Justina and his fishermen uncles, and would have been destined, like most of the poor children around him in the streets of Iquique, to a life extracting *mariscos* from the sea if he had not felt compelled, at a very early age, to read every book he could get his hands on. These were the two worlds he would always carry with him, on the one hand, the rough and tumble domain of street fighting and obscenities and not knowing where the next meal might come from, and on the other hand the highbrow realm of intellect and revolution. Two worlds which Freddy never had any trouble reconciling or, at least juxtaposing, from an early age. There was a rock that Jinny had told me about, just off one of Iquique's coves, a large craggy blackish boulder that I had stood on just a few days ago, where each dawn Freddy would do his homework. It was his outdoor desk. But he also used it to crack open the shellfish he caught in that same bay a bit after he had finished his school tasks and that would often constitute his only repast of the day. He had never tried to hide who he was or where he came from, never tried to make himself over, Eliza Doolittle-like, into something he was not. I had seen him myself, in the days of our successful Student Union campaigns, attack his adversaries with a slew of the most flagrant vulgarities and then suddenly switch to the most sophisticated Marxist philosophical arguments. This effortless shuttle between writing complex papers about the Aymara Indians and their influence on the Norte Grande and deeply understanding the impoverished and unlettered life that most Chileans lived had stood him in good stead in our political work together in the shantytowns of Santiago, but I had not anticipated—indeed did not even know about—how it affected his image in his native Iquique. The first working-class child in the neighborhood to ever make it to the university, he had become a legend back home, and when he returned each summer—to work in menial jobs and continue his diving expeditions for food—his train was invariably received by flocks of young boys who would follow him around as if he were some sort of boxing champion. It was this charisma that had allowed him, one summer, to call together, according to Senén Durán, all the experts on the word Iquique and shut them in a room and refuse them food—but not drink!—until they had come up with the unanimous opinion that the word derived from the Aymara for a place where the seabirds come to sleep.

So that was Freddy: popular and brainy, humorous and analytical, forceful and brave, easy with people and comfortable with scholarly research, ready to fight with his fists and ready to fight with his mouth. Almost bilingual, crossing effortlessly from the language of the street-smart kid to that of the academic genius. I am aware of the peril of overidealizing anybody from the dangerous distance of death. I certainly had differences with him back then and might have them now if we sat down to argue heatedly as we used to in our student days. He had always seemed to me, in spite of a real veneration for democracy and Allende in particular, to be excessively obsessed with the ultimate need for armed violence if the poor were ever to really change their lot, even in our Chilean revolution that had proclaimed a peaceful road to socialism. A revolutionary process that would give my friend space to mature and grow, show his talents as a natural leader. Not entirely an anomaly, Freddy, in a country where the whole working class of which he was a member was rising out of poverty and powerlessness and had started to govern with Allende in 1970, the first president in Chile who had ever named a textile worker to be minister of labor and a peasant to be minister of agriculture. Making Freddy Taberna at the age of twenty-seven and already back in his native Iquique one of the most powerful men in the Norte Grande—the man who headed the president's socialist party in the province and also in charge of Odeplan, something like the regional Ministry of Economy.

Indeed, it was that important post which had offered him a challenge that reveals, perhaps more than any other incident, his caliber as a human being. "One day," Jinny told me in Santiago, "it must have been in 1972, the doorbell rings at home and I open the door and right there in front of me is Freddy's father." She had recognized him because one day, on the street, some months after they had arrived in Iquique in 1967, Freddy had shown her a man—*you see that guy over there, that's my father.* She was astonished. *So you know him?* she had asked. *Never met him,* was Freddy's response. Jinny had suggested that Freddy go up to the man who had deserted his mother and never cared about him, the father who owned a couple of trucks but had never offered the slightest help to his son. Freddy had refused to even say hello, merely shrugged his shoulders. *It's all the same to me. Never talked to him before, don't need to talk to him now.*

"And now," Jinny told me, "there he was. And the father asks: 'Does *el Señor Taberna* happen to be in?' I told him to wait, went to get Freddy and said, 'It's your dad. He's at the door.' *What does he want?* 'He asked for *el Señor Taberna*.'" Calling Freddy by the name of his stepfather, the name Freddy had taken from his stepfather.

"*What can I do for you?* Freddy told him to come in, to take a seat, how could he be of assistance? Typical of Freddy—to understand others, what they might be going through, to put his own father at ease, not be judgmental with him. His father had said that he really had not wanted to bother *el Señor Taberna*, very timidly suggested that he had some problems."

It was a time when the U.S. economic blockade against Allende's government and internal sabotage had created a serious shortage of parts for machines and vehicles—and it was Odeplan, which Freddy directed, that determined the distribution of those valuable spare parts. Jinny watched them from a corner of the room, not noticing anything special going on between them, talking like any two adults who had never met before, two strangers with nothing special joining them, no allusion to the many times the father had seen the son cleaning fishing boats, waxing the floors of houses, washing windows, passed the boy on the street without so much as a nod. "After his father left," Jinny had continued, "I told Freddy to send him to *la punta del cerro* [the equivalent of sending him to hell]. *Of course not*, Freddy said. *I'll help him like I'd help anyone in need.*"

Unselfish and generous Freddy.

Which should not be confused with softness, any sense that he would be flexible and easygoing with the enemies of the revolution. In those tense, confrontational times, as the military coup approached, Freddy had made many enemies and was targeted as one of the most menacing members of the local government. Indeed, a friend from Antofagasta—Eugenio Ruiz Tagle, who was himself to be horribly tortured and mutilated after the coup—had warned Freddy that the army had plans to kill him if they took power, Eugenio had overheard General Forestier, the regional commander, mention Freddy Taberna as the first one they would have to eliminate.

When I heard this story, first from Jinny and then from Lautaro Núñez, I wondered whether Pinochet had not been behind that decision, if they had any proof or rumor about the dictator's participation in Freddy's execution, and both Jinny and Lautaro had said that all they had were suspicions.

But Pinochet had indeed given the order to murder Freddy, a responsibility that Angélica and I had discovered, entirely by chance, on this trip. And the informant had been, bizarre as this may seem, Angélica's Aunt Laura Müller. She had been close to the Pinochet family, visiting them often and playing bridge with his wife, Lucía Hiriart, back in the early sixties when *el General* was in charge of the local Iquique regiment and Laura had been a judge on the appellate court. And later, when Pinochet, now the strongman of Chile, toured Iquique—his favorite city in the world!—in the mid-seventies, Laura and the dictator met, cordially it seems, according to our new friend Ivor who, the night we had dined at his house, recounted Laura's version of that conversation.

Although Ivor did not want to hurt Laura by bringing up the painful past, he felt that it was impossible to avoid asking her how she could sit down to have a drink with the dictator of Chile when her own son Fernando had died in—Ivor used the term *condiciones extrañas*—strange circumstances, a safe way of alluding to the murder of Fernando.

It was clear from Laura's answer to Ivor that she was in denial, refused to blame the military for the death of her almost blind son Fernando a few years after the coup. Because Laura changed the subject. "I used the opportunity to ask Pinochet something else," she said. "I asked him: Why did you kill Freddy Taberna?"

Ivor explained that Laura Müller had known Freddy since he was a tot, that she had always kept an eye on him, had liked him immensely. Or maybe she was really demanding to know about her son, wanted to ask about Fernando and asked about Freddy instead.

Pinochet was not, in any case, a man for subtleties of interpretation, and had answered: "And what the hell did you want me to do, Laurita? Wait for him to command the resistance, that he take up arms and lead the revolt against me? You know what sort of leader he could have become. *Tuve que matarlo.* I had to kill him."

Though it turned out not to be that easy.

The day of the coup, September 11, 1973, Freddy had gone into clandestinity—flitting from house to house, trying to hide what was an imposing physique. Freddy was tall, skinny, exceedingly agile and muscular, with striking features that I had always felt were primarily indigenous, though on this trip

I discovered that he owed much more to his Croatian maternal grandfather—at any rate, Freddy was immediately recognizable, even after he had shaved his unkempt beard and shorn his scraggly hair. If the military, with their incessant raids, were unable to find him, it was because he had finally been given refuge by the Padres Oblatos, members of the very order of priests that had created the first kindergarten in the pampas in Humberstone in the 1930s—and whose father superior, a Canadian citizen, would pay dearly for having taken Freddy in. The army had arrested him, driven him to the Peruvian frontier, and thrown him across the border. There in Tacna that priest had cried the loss of the country he had come to consider his own.

Freddy's fate would, of course, be worse than exile. He was forced to turn himself in when the army arrested Jinny six days after the coup, spreading the false rumor that she was being gang-raped in the local regiment while their two children, Nacho (age three) and Daniela (age one) were living in utter abandonment (also not true, as they had first been cared for by Oscar Varela and his wife and then by Jinny's mother and sister, who had come from their native La Serena to help).

They let Jinny go when Freddy was arrested, but she would soon be detained again. Not, however, before she managed to find a lawyer who would defend her husband—a difficult task, as Freddy was being held incommunicado in a sort of container, broiling under the hot Iquique sun, where he was tortured for days on end. Before the military came for her, she had seen Freddy for one last time. From afar. She had been waiting outside the military headquarters where they would take Freddy for his daily interrogations and her patience had paid off, because one day she caught a glimpse of him. Jinny shouted and Freddy turned and smiled and made a gesture with his hand, as if to say, I'm all right, take care.

But he was the one who needed to take care.

He was the one who ended up, one month later, here in Pisagua, accused of sedition and betrayal of the Fatherland in front of a military tribunal. To make matters worse, the prosecuting lawyer (*fiscal militar*) was none other than Mario Acuña, a man whom Freddy had publicly denounced as a criminal just a few weeks before the coup, a well-known drug trafficker who also dabbled in smuggling and black-marketeering in those turbulent economic times. Acuña had already begun settling scores. Oscar Varela—an apolitical fishing expert who had been arrested and ended up in Pisagua as well only because he was Freddy's friend—was allowed to go out on the bay every morning with a sergeant to dive for shellfish, a delicacy much appreciated by the military officers, and from that vantage point had witnessed the execution on the other side of the harbor of four of Acuña's accomplices in the drug trade.

And now Acuña had Freddy Taberna at his mercy.

And almost thirty years later, here I was, visiting the place where Freddy's verdict had been delivered, where he had said good-bye to his brother, where he had prepared himself for what was to come.

I had been anticipating my own night here in Pisagua ever since I decided to come to the Norte Grande to write this book, I had thought that perhaps I would spend the hours until dawn in a vigil, watching from outside the prison or from inside the

Pisagua Hotel: The hotel owner standing outside her kitchen in the former prison courtyard

hotel, separated from the prison that had held Freddy by only a mere couple of meters, by nothing more significant than a balustrade, I had prepared myself for some sort of mourning ceremony, but as I mounted the steps to our room—and again that wave of rotten smell washed over me—I had a vision of Freddy laughing at me, saying to me *no seái huevón*, don't be a fool, you'll need your energies tomorrow, Ariel, and I smiled back at him and fell into a dreamless sleep, awaking to this Saturday when I will explore the prison quarters before crossing the sloping bay to the cemetery where Freddy faced that firing squad.

This, then, is the central quad where, on the night of October 29, 1973, at exactly ten o'clock at night, Lt. Col. Ramón Larraín had spoken to the prisoners, demanding their attention. "We were locked in our cells on the upper floor," Oscar Varela had explained to us in his home in Iquique, "so we couldn't see the officer, no matter how hard we pressed against the bars. Nor see Freddy and the others, either."

Angélica and I climb the wooden stairs to the third story of the prison and we understand what Oscar meant. The over-crowded cells—five hundred political prisoners in a penitentiary built for sixty convicts—are half a meter back from the walkways and the railings that wrap around the inside of the jailhouse and gape out onto the empty space above the inner patio where Larraín started to announce the sentences dictated by the military tribunals. I crane my neck, try to see what those men might have seen: Only the hotel was incongruously visible from here, the bougainvillea blooming gloriously. So those five hundred men had been forced to hear Larraín call out the names of the ten hostages who were to be executed the next day at dawn, they had been very quiet trying to listen to how the condemned men who were formed below in the patio had reacted, but not another sound had come up through the void. "Maybe," Oscar had said, "come to think of it, Freddy was still in his cell." And when Larraín had returned an hour later and declared that he had managed to have six of the ten sentences commuted to life in prison, there was hope that, in the end, Freddy and his three compañeros would be spared as well.

But a few minutes later soldiers had begun to glue crosses, cut from strips of plastic gauze, on the wall next to each cell, each recruit trying to avert his eyes from the eyes of the prisoners, and then, from the bottom of the stairs, from the patio where Larraín had made his announcements, the voice of the military chaplain flown in that morning had been heard rising, a Mass for the four men who were about to die and who had themselves listened to those prayers from their own small units where they were held in solitary confinement.

That was where Angélica and I ventured next, down to the ground floor, stopping again in front of that large door to one side of the quad that Freddy had occupied, according to Pichón. The solitary door had been tightly shut that night, but it now opened soundlessly and I enter that orderly, brightly repainted room, close the door behind me, watch the light streaming in from vertical bars above that door. Much too high for Freddy to have looked out. Nor would he have been able to lift himself up to see through the large window on the back wall, from where the sound of the sea now wafted in, perhaps that night there had been a breeze like today.

Pisagua Hotel: Freddy Taberna's cell

It had been from here that Freddy started to sing songs, Oscar Varela had told us that all night long they could hear Freddy singing. The other three condemned men had been more silent. Larraín had given them paper and pen so they could write letters to their loved ones. But Freddy had refused that offer from his jailer. According to Jinny, he did not want her to spend the rest of her life reading the last letter he had ever written. He had sent her a message, "that I knew how he loved me," and Jinny's voice was as calm as she told me this story in Santiago as when we had first spoken in the Toronto of our common exile in the early eighties, "and he knew how much I would suffer with his death, what would happen to me. But that I was a strong woman and would find a better compañero than him to share my life with. *Que me recordará los dos juntos, así como habíamos vivido.* To always remember him together with her, both of them, just as they had lived."

We know that these were Freddy's final words to his wife, because his half-brother, Pichón, was called by a soldier outside his cell sometime before midnight on that October 29: "Taberna, Héctor Taberna."

"*Presente!*"

"Your brother wants to speak to you."

Pichón had told me about that farewell conversation with Freddy two days ago, on my last night in Iquique, Thursday, May 23. It was hard for us to join up because Héctor Taberna sleeps all day and works at the casino until daybreak as an inspector—a job only offered to him once democracy returned to Chile because during the seventeen years of the dictatorship he had been systematically blackballed by the authorities, he said, due to his blood ties with Freddy. So it was at the casino that we finally hooked up, just Pichón and me, because Angélica had insisted that I go by myself, that Pichón would be more forthcoming. As usual, she was right—one of the first things Pichón had told me was that he had spoken to Freddy's picture before leaving for work that evening: "I'm going to see your old friend Ariel Dorfman," he had said. This was a ritual he had perfected over the years, speaking to Freddy every time he went out, hoping this would bring him luck. He had always been in awe of that brother six years his senior, who had accomplished what nobody else in Iquique had even dared to dream: a poor fisherboy, who had a university degree and had been one of the geographers who had set the limits with Argentina when there had been a frontier conflict and had been given a scholarship to the United States and been head of the Student Union and Odeplan and ...

There was something uncanny, almost shocking, about Pichón, the way in which he resembled his brother, the hawk-like nose, the long hair, the tall body. I had not seen Freddy for almost forty years, not even a likeness, and the image that I had stored and shaped and softened in my mind over this time was not at all like the Freddy of the photos that Jinny and Oscar and Leyla and Lautaro and other friends had been showing me these last few weeks. It wasn't that Pichón was a ringer for his brother. He was less handsome and the almond eyes more watery-red and the hair with streaks of white and the nose flatter now that I looked more carefully, but he brought back to me in a rush the flesh and blood, warmth and color of the Freddy I had known and loved, much more than the cold photographs that had distanced my friend and didn't fit into my memories. It was as if a slightly altered replica of Freddy was returning to my life at the exact moment when I most needed him, when I was on the verge of hearing the story of his last encounter with his family, ready to hear it from this younger brother.

"I had come running down the stairs and they open the cell and I see Freddy and I throw myself into his arms and I hug him so hard so hard ..." and here, Pichón wrapped his arms and hands around his torso as if he were Freddy, as if Freddy were right there next to the chairs where we sat in the casino of Iquique, just a few steps away from where the roulette tables whirl and the blackjack dealers expound their aces and sevens and kings, "and he calms me, he begins to caress my hair, which was just as long as it is now, till I'm better, *calm down, calm down,* and now I can separate myself from him and I see his face, I see the marks of where they've tortured him and he is so whole, so full of dignity, *tan íntegro,* and he says that it's all right, that the struggle will go on, that I have to wait five years, to lay low for five years and then go back and start fighting again, and I can't believe that he is the one giving me courage, he is making sure I tell the other compañeros not to be sad and not to be afraid. And then he gave me his watch."

"And then what?"

"We didn't sleep all night. We could hear Freddy singing and then just before dawn, they took them out and then we managed to see him as he left and he had his fist up high."

"And is there anything else he said to you?"

"Just that the accusations against him were all false and the trial was illegal and also ..."

"Also?"

"*Ojalá que no me duela*. I hope it won't hurt."

I breathed hard at that. It was easier to deal with a heroic Freddy, a super Freddy, rather than the ordinary, normal Freddy who, like anybody on this planet, would dread the horrible death that awaited him. A Freddy who allowed himself, if even for a moment, to show fear. It brought me so close to him, that fear of pain that must have come out of whatever had been viciously inflicted upon him day to day and night after night in the different dungeons where he had been kept. And I felt overwhelmed by the reality of what he must have been thinking and living, I had an irresistible urge to be embraced, to embrace Freddy, Pichón, somebody, anybody.

There welled up inside me at that moment something that Jinny had recounted to me in Santiago and that I had tried to forget, had not wanted to examine too intimately at the time. The year that had followed Freddy's death had been spent, according to Jinny, in a fog. What she knows about that period comes from her mother, her sister, her friends, but she personally recalls not one moment. If she slowly climbed out of the madness and depression into which she had been plunged by the news of Freddy's execution, it was because she had started to help other women whose husbands had been killed or disappeared and, above all, because she needed to care for the children. Psychologists had given her what she now thinks was flawed advice, that she not reveal to her eldest boy or the younger daughter the fate of their father. She would tell Nacho—who was the first to ask, the first to realize that he did not, like most other children around him, have a daddy—that

Freddy was traveling, or that he'd gone abroad and would someday return, lying to the boy to spare him sorrow, perhaps lying to herself as well. Until one day in Santiago some years after Freddy's assassination, walking along Tobalaba, an ample avenue laced with leafy trees that borders a large flowing canal of green water, Jinny decided to tell the child the truth.

Nachito, do you know that your father is dead?

How did he die?

The military killed him.

How did they kill him?

They shot him.

In the heart?

Yes.

And did it hurt him?

Jinny didn't answer and Nacho never asked again.

So much more comfortable to think of Freddy singing as they readied the rifles, so difficult to concentrate on the moment when those bullets reached his body. Because Jinny had also told me that the soldiers in the firing squad had been ordinary conscripts, not very good shooters, and that when they botched the job it was Espinoza Davies, a captain who would later gain notoriety as the head of one of Pinochet's torture centers, who had gone over to the riddled body of Freddy and shot him point-blank with an army pistol.

All that pain coming back to me, flooding me all over again, in the casino in Iquique, what I had wanted to erase from my own memory and that Pichón's words had forced back to the surface of my mind.

Our conversation was coming to a close.

Somebody had interrupted us, warned Pichón that he was needed at one of the gambling tables. Pichón had looked at me disconsolately. "I've been carrying him ever since, you know? Like a backpack I've been carrying him. Living so he would be proud of me."

There was such a welter of sadness swirling in him, such a skin of vulnerability, that I suddenly understood why Héctor Taberna had been nicknamed *pichón* as a child, called that way, perhaps by Freddy himself. Pichón, which means a little bird, a bird that is just hatched and needs protection. Still hungering for his dead and mythical brother, ravaged by that death, unable to pick up the pieces of his own life.

I felt he expected me to say something.

"I'm sure you can carry him," I replied. "You're the elder brother now, right? He'll always stay like that, the age he was when they killed him. But you—you have to keep growing, be the head of the family."

He was silent for a few seconds. Then: "You think that's what Freddy would have said to me?"

"Maybe."

He nodded. "I'll say hello to Freddy when I go back home tomorrow morning, tell him I saw you." Pichón hesitated and then, like a final gift, an offering to his brother's friend, he added: "You know, Freddy used to come into the house. He would come in lifting up the lids of the pots and pans and smell what was cooking. And the day they killed him—it was October 30 and that last night before he…, Freddy had remembered that it would be our mother's birthday, asked me to tell Mom that he had not forgotten that day…. Well, on

October 30, not too late in the morning, the lids began to jump off the pots that were boiling over, and I think that Freddy came to say good-bye to Mom, that's what I think."

As for me in Pisagua this Saturday, I need to get out of this jailroom that Pichón described to me in such excruciating detail. I suddenly feel sick of this penitentiary, sick of this hotel, sick of those dense dirty white walls, anxious to finally arrive at that place where Freddy had been killed and that was there, on the other side of the sparkling blue bay, waiting for me.

One more little detour.

First we picked up Rafael Gaete and his wife, Katerine Saldaña, a couple of Allendistas who had moved to Pisagua from their exile in Canada some years ago to try and restore its monuments, and walked through town with them. We needed to see how drained and quiet and cursed its inhabitants are, nobody speaking out, nobody looking you in the eye, a town that had promised itself in the nineteenth century to be open and energetic like Iquique and had ended up frustrated and bitter and wary. Getting our hosts to show us the most marvelous Teatro Municipal of all the ghost towns visited because this one is built not in the desert but directly on the sea and its waves pound on the back, crash against the farthest wall of the theater itself—but even this wondrous spectacle, the gem of Pisagua, turns out to be tainted, even this architectural portent lives under the shadow of a defilement. Katerine invites us to mount to the second floor of the reception hall in the adjoining building, where the ladies and gentlemen of yesteryear's salitre boom once sipped their cocktails before *La Traviata* was performed and where, almost a century later, hundreds of jailed women, political prisoners segregated from the male population of the penitentiary, slept and ate and pissed and tried to smuggle out messages, these ruined chambers where on certain days those women would hear shots from the other side of the bay and guess that another execution was taking place. A perfect way to finish our visit to Pisagua. Historic Pisagua, malevolent old Pisagua, Pisagua which tourists avoid like the plague, which Katerine has hopes for and will try to save for the future. The same Pisagua through which Freddy had been driven in that truck or that jeep or whatever the hell they had used to move him and his three compañeros, the same route we follow now skirting the bay for a couple of miles, and yes, here we are, here is this cemetery isolated from any house or inkling of habitation, its crosses jutting out of the sand and brown gray rock as if they were malevolent toothpicks, here I am at this place of death that I have been trying to imagine ever since I received the news of Freddy's death nearly thirty years ago.

Rafael takes us to the *fosa,* the long and deep and wide pit where the remains of nineteen political prisoners had been discovered. The names are listed, flowers are strewn in the sand and stone that surround its yawning depths, the inevitable verses from Neruda are carved into the rock. I have seen dozens of similar sites all over Chile. We visited one, in fact, less than a week ago, just outside Calama, on our way back from San Pedro, a barren slope where yet other friends of ours had been executed in the aftermath of the coup, that strip of sun-baked desert more forlorn and cheerless than this one because at least the ocean is here, at least here some bodies were found.

Pisagua's cemetery

Freddy was not among them. There are many others like him in Chile, the infamous *desaparecidos* whose bodies were never returned to their families for burial after they were killed. Most of those dissidents were kidnapped, their arrest and whereabouts denied by the secret police, consigning their relatives to an inferno of perpetual uncertainty. What differentiates Freddy and a few select others is that, in their case, the military admitted the murder, allowing their families the absurd consolation of knowing that their loved ones had really died. Unlike other women, Jinny did not have to imagine her husband in some dank hole being incessantly beaten or starved, did not have to spend the rest of her life hoping he would come home and oh so slowly realizing that this return or resurrection was impossible. This is her one sad advantage: Jinny has been told how Freddy was killed.

Calama: Cross marking a mass grave of desaparecidos

How strange that the person who first informed the world about the circumstances of that death was to be Lt. Col. Ramón Larraín, that I should have to evoke his words now in order to conjure up what happened here.

Larraín had returned to the prison an hour or so after the execution on that morning of October 30, 1973, and—according to everyone I have talked to, Jinny and Oscar and Pichón and Lautaro—he had once again spoken to the prisoners from the inner patio, his voice resonating through every cell of the penitentiary. Larraín had informed them that Freddy Taberna was the most valiant man he had ever encountered and every Chilean soldier should be that brave. The army officer who had carried out the orders to put Freddy to death had been turned by Freddy's valor into the bearer of the story of that death. Larraín's version, still haunting us: Freddy had refused to be injected with a drug that would numb him, had asked that the blindfold be lifted from his eyes, had begun to sing a song, "La Marseillaise," as they placed him against the wall of rocks opposite the beach. And then, just before the bullets hit him, Larraín reported, Freddy had shouted out the words: "*No nos acallarán. Venceremos.* They will not silence us. We shall overcome."

And yet it was the very Larraín who had provided an ending to the story of Freddy's life who had also left that story gaping open like a wound, it had been Larraín himself who had made sure that Freddy's body would disappear. Denying closure to Jinny and her children, refusing to Pichón the reprieve and relief of a burial ceremony, depriving those who survived Freddy of our right to mourn him. Forcing a search that has continued to this day.

The first person who returned to Pisagua after the execution, to this very spot where I now stand, had been Oscar Varela, who, five years later—on his return from the inner exile in Arica to which he had been banished once the military freed him from prison—took his wife, Leyla, to show her where their Freddy had died, see if there was any clue to where the body might be hidden. But a few months before twenty campesinos from the central valley of Santiago had been discovered in an abandoned mine in Lonquén, thirty kilometers from Chile's capital, and, as a result of that first scandalous uncovering of the remains of missing men whose arrest had always been denied, the military had initiated an operation all over the country to clean up every site where a massacre or an execution had taken place. It was, Oscar said, as if a wind had swept everything away, all traces of the crime and even of the concentration camp built by the prisoners in the months after Freddy's death, erased by the soldiers. A couple of *mariscadores*, young men who were diving for shellfish, said they had seen human bones in a cavern near the bottom of the bay, in a cove that, when I turn my head slightly to the north, I can see now gleaming whitely under the sun. But nothing could be done back then. The military were still watching, attentive and alert, and had battered to within an inch of his life a man called Choque, a Chilean deep-sea diver who had won a medal at the Olympics and who had been imprudent enough to talk in a bar about corpses he had spotted one afternoon off one of the beaches of Pisagua.

It was only when democracy returned in 1990 that a group of Freddy's friends felt free enough to search for the body. After many false starts and leads—for a while they had dug up the beach of pebbles that is a hundred yards below where Freddy was finished off—they had at length found, on this terrace next to the cemetery where I am at this moment observing the landscape, a patch of earth which seemed softer, along with the year 1973 carved enigmatically into a rock. It was only then that Lautaro Núñez had been called in as an expert and they had opened that mass grave.

And all those bones had appeared, tightly packed, one on top of the other in sacks. All those bones, but no Freddy.

What had happened to him?

Where should I look?

I am inhabited by voices. Everybody I have talked to has a different version, an echo of the rumors that flowed over the years, each new story leading to yet another search or excavation, a renewed hope that Freddy would be found. Ricardo

Núñez recalled a cove closer to Pisagua, near the dock where I had walked last night for a while. Sergio Bitar told me about someone who had called him asking for money in return for a tip as to where Freddy's body had been concealed. Oscar thinks that first they buried Freddy and then later on took him out of the pit and made him disappear. And Pichón insisted that they had dynamited his brother's body and that it will be found soon at the bottom of a ravine to the north of the cemetery. And then there is Jinny, who told me of the horror of days and days of digging up the sands with special excavating machines brought in by an investigating judge, Jinny who had said that this was the worst thing that had happened to her since Freddy's death, the whole flat esplanade where I now stand and that looks almost like the beehive of an exhausted nitrate field filled with perforations and holes and the gaping sore of the *fosa*.... And Rafael, our host this morning in Pisagua, telling us that the rumors in town are that the military buried the bodies in the cemetery itself—what better place to hide a corpse, what solution could be more perverse?

But it is finally Lautaro's words that come back to me, guide me as I wander up and down this killing field where I know I will find nothing:

"We began to look for a place where a helicopter might land. And with a master builder who was helping with the investigation, ten meters from where there were fibers that indicated that a canvas had covered the bodies, we found residues of sand and cement. The only remnants of cement in the surrounding five kilometers. So any archaeologist can conjure up the image: soldiers, ten meters from the body, mixing cement and sand. For what? To weigh the body down, make sure it will sink to the bottom of the sea when they throw it from the helicopter."

They cast him into the sea.

Now Rafael takes me to the rock where we can still see the bullet marks, against which Freddy and the others stood, one by one by one.

I do not move.

Rafael and Angélica discreetly leave me, decide to explore the nearby cemetery. She makes a gesture to me. Rafael needs to return to Pisagua, where Katerine is preparing lunch—and we need to start on the last leg of our journey, arrive tonight in Arica.

I nod. I will not be long.

So this is what Freddy Taberna saw, these wild waves, this desolate cove, these thousand crosses of a cemetery two centuries old, this is the last thing Freddy saw when they slipped the blindfold from his eyes, his last landscape before the bullets from the firing squad reached him.

This is where Freddy heard Larraín give the order to fire.

I try to make the place speak to me. To tell me where the helicopter landed. For these rocks to reveal what they saw, their secrets. I can't help it: What my eyes fix on next, closer to the beach, is another sort of huella, the recent footprint that a dog left in the sand. There is something so real about this place that has been described to me so many times over and yet so hollow, dry inside, not a drop of water or mercy to be pressed out of these indifferent stones.

Where is he? Where is Freddy?

Strange, so strange, that I may know Freddy now, in death, more than I ever did when we communed with the gardens and the air and the struggles of Santiago. Strange that if he had not died, I would not have recovered him in this way. Strange that it is his death which delivers him back to us as a challenge.

No, it is not here I will find Freddy.

I would rather remember the trace he left behind somewhere else, some place he would smile at.

There is a street in Iquique which bears his name. Calle Freddy Taberna. Every morning at dawn—come to think of it, more or less at the time that he had been facing the firing squad right here in Pisagua ... Early so early when I like to take my morning walks, that was when I would cross the ten or so blocks from our hotel to the tumultuous rocks and waves at the inlet where he used to plunge in the waters and come up with his meal of the day, I would stop there next to the Pacific for some minutes, breathe deeply and do some meditation and yoga, and from there walk up the street. Starting at the Court of Appeals that overlooks the ocean and continuing five blocks east, toward the mountains, ending in a school where young men and women were streaming into the same building Freddy had attended. Like Iquique itself, those five blocks are full of life, a mix of different residences and styles of life, ramshackle houses and large mansions, from the time of the nitrate boom and from the poverty of the nitrate bust.

Calle Freddy Taberna 14. Calle Freddy Taberna 45. Calle Freddy Taberna 133.

I like to think of letters being sent from near and far to those who live and love and work on Freddy's street, the barrio of El Morro in Iquique where he himself played and wandered as a child without ever knowing that he would end up in that sea he loved so well or that he himself would refuse to send one last letter. The essence of Freddy: that he never wanted his life or his story to be closed, finished, over. That he was always on the move, hoping for something better for himself and everyone around him. Yes, that's how I want him to be remembered, all those people receiving letters with his name on the envelope, all those men and women, old and young and children sitting down to write letters themselves with that return address on the back, Freddy Taberna, *nuestro Freddy,* our Freddy, a street in Iquique where life simply goes on.

EPILOGUE

Footsteps in the North: Arica and Beyond

I am sitting at my desk in Durham, North Carolina, many months after I apparently left the desert, many miles to the north of that North of Chile, I sit here finishing this book and wondering where it led me, that journey into my multiple origins, here I am, asking myself what I finally brought back from the desert, trying to figure out what remains of that trip.

It was supposed to end, that trip, in the Arica where the desert comes to its own end and where another part of America has its beginning—and in a sense, that is what happened, our physical journey did conclude when on May 27 Angélica and I, honoring a family superstition, each boarded separate planes back to Santiago.

But the desert has a way of staying with you even if your body has departed; the desert's stories, having found a foothold in our memory, did not leave us alone, would never again, in some sense, leave us alone.

Over the following months we heard from many of the men and women who had accompanied our odyssey.

Mario Pino Quivira tells me that a Chilean foundation has approved a grant to secure the artifacts rescued from Monte Verde, so that in the near future the huella that has survived thirteen thousand years of inclement weather will be protected from the human depredations of the twenty-first century. Although money is, of course, still not forthcoming for the project, an architect has already drawn up plans for the museum that will grace the site.

And from San Pedro de Atacama, Carolina Agüero—who is adding a master's degree in anthropology to her already impressive credentials—lets me know something I never thought to ask when we visited her: It turns out she had been working in Monte Verde as a student intern that day in 1983 when the footprint was found, her eyes had been among the first to see its recovery, her hands had taken it to Santiago for its first examination.

And, in other news from San Pedro, we hear that Lautaro Núñez has been given the maximum honor a historian can receive in Chile, the National Prize for History, a belated recognition of someone who has helped change the way in which Chileans view their own past.

And Miguel Roth sends me gossip from Las Campanas, about the universe and the astronomers and his own struggle against loneliness.

And I hear from our hosts in Chuquicamata that the

evacuation is proceeding according to schedule and the rubble is waiting to fall upon the town and the graveyard will be spared.

And Julio Valdivia is still waiting behind his desk in Humberstone for UNESCO to approve the *salitreras* as a patrimony of humanity, while at night he chases away marauders who would steal the pino de oregón and steal his memories and steal his dreams.

And Hernán Rivera Letelier has published a novel on the massacre at Santa María de Iquique, the story of a love affair that manages to guiltily flourish at the very moment when the blood starts to flow.

And Eduardo Riquelme continues to spend his weekends in the abandoned oficinas in the pampas and prepares for the Day of the Dead, when he will visit the tomb of a child and the tomb of an adult and remember them in the middle of the desert.

And Rafael Gaete and Katerine Saldaña have selected a plot in the cemetery of Pisagua, the one place in Chile where they won't have to pay for a grave, hoping to be bound together in death as they were in life.

And Sergio Bitar, who has been named minister of education.

All those friends, old and recent, who refuse to disappear, who send us information from time to time, all those friends answered by our own updates, our own news.

And then, of course, there are the dead themselves.

They have also found a way to re-emerge into our existence.

Starting with Freddy Taberna.

In Santiago, a few days after our return from the Norte Grande and just before we left for Buenos Aires, I was lucky enough to find Jinny at home with all her family. She had not told me, out of delicacy, that she was celebrating her birthday, but on the way to the apartment, I had picked up some flowers—maybe Freddy was the one who had whispered to me that I should bring some sort of offering. He had, at any rate, some surprises in store for me. One was a story about Freddy that his own children had never heard and that Jinny told me when she heard that I was puzzled that Freddy's life had swung between the two extremes of the coast and the mountains, the sea to which he and his uncles had been born, and the Andean highlands and indigenous population that he had spent most of his youth studying. What I could not figure out was why the desert in between seemed to be of no interest to him; in all the conversations I had held with all those friends of his, not once had any mention been made of a connection to the nitrate cycle that was so crucial to the history of Iquique. Jinny had filled in one more empty space in the lost story, had revealed that, as a boy of eight or nine, Freddy would make some pesos by going up to the abandoned ghost towns to help dismantle houses, working side by side with men who were destroying the very places that had once sheltered their caliche dreams, Freddy listening at night to their stories of exploitation and suffering and struggle, Freddy tearing down memories as a child and trying to keep them alive as an adult. So Freddy had also been affected, like everyone else I had met in the North of Chile, by the enormous tragedy of the salitre, perhaps he had sworn to himself in those long nights in the desert that his children would know a different fate.

And that was the other surprise Freddy had arranged for me on this visit—those wonderful children, Daniela and Nacho, who had hardly known their father and even so managed to bring him back to me almost miraculously. Nacho, in particular, at one point in our conversation, responded to one of my fancy theories about the North with a gesture—but it was more than just a gesture, it was an attitude. Something indefinable exuded from Nacho, a sort of self-confidence, a *"desplante,"* we would call it in Spanish, a way of looking straight at you and not accepting immediately what you're saying. Not that he was suspicious, but rather that Nacho was measuring you, challenging you, like Freddy always did, to back up with deeds any words you might utter. Reminding me more of my dead friend than any photo or even his amazing reincarnation in Pichón. That fluttering of Nacho's hands that I had not seen in thirty-five years—that was how Freddy had moved his arms, that was how Freddy had jutted his jaw out just a bit, that was Freddy up and down, suddenly and entirely in front of me one more time. So without my ever being aware of it, he has been inside me all these decades, in some hiding place of memory, lodged in who knows what gonads or neurons, waiting to be jolted into visibility by the faraway surviving son.

Ways in which the past persists.

Like the Müllers in Angélica, like the Malinarich lineage.

Because they also have made a dramatic reappearance in our lives, those forefathers and foremothers of Angélica's began flaring back into her existence in ways that we could not have imagined when we grappled with the faint traces they left behind in Iquique.

In Buenos Aires, the city where I was born and where my ninety-five-year-old father and other relatives still live, and where—the day after our arrival—we are blessed with the dramatic bombshell discovery that we had prayed for during our frantic search in Iquique.

We find Angélica's grandfather Angel Malinarich Pinto.

Well, not the man personally, not in flesh and blood. He did, after all, die in 1974 in Buenos Aires. Though it is not true that he had come directly to the capital of Argentina. His first thirty years away from home had been spent just across the Andes, in Mendoza, where he arrived by train on May 23, 1918, with his sister-in-law, Rosa, and where they were soon joined by his mother, Carmela Pinto Benavides, and where his illegitimate son, Rodolfo, was born. And we have photos of him and his mother standing in front of a house! And she is far darker than we had ever thought she would be and he is far lighter. And other photos, some where he reminds us of our son Rodrigo and some where he seems an entire stranger. And a record he made for that mother many years later, singing happy birthday to her, reciting a poem he had composed for Mother's Day. And we know that he squandered his fortune on elusive mining ventures in Mendoza. And we have discovered the name of his father, which is Ruperto Francisco, the nephew who came from Croatia and inherited the fortune of the Malinarich brothers, the fortune which would allow his son to escape to Argentina and never work for the rest of his life. And more, so much more—how Angel Malinarich was charming and seductive and something of a con man, how he used his forging skills to make false documents for his Bolshevik buddies, how he married several more times and begat many children, how he hocked the furs he gave to one of his wives, how he never forgot his native land and consorted with famous Chilean singers of boleros in Argentina and sang with them and danced away whole nights and ... After trying to crush information out of the stone hard desert of the Norte Grande, this is like an avalanche, a rainstorm, a forest of data and dates and names, such a cornucopia of stories that I would need another book to tell them rather than this book that is drawing to its close.

And all of this is now known to us because we have found something far more important than the story of the lost grandfather. We have found his family. We have visited the house in San Fernando, a river town just outside Buenos Aires, where he spent the last twenty-five years of his life, where two of his four children live, where the last of the wives he wed in Argentina also greets us.

It was just a matter of looking up the name Malinarich in the phone book and making calls, that is how simple it is, that is how simple it could have been to speak to him the first time Angélica visited Argentina with me and my parents in 1964, meet him on any of our subsequent visits. He was, in fact, still alive when we passed through here in 1973 on our way to exile. We might have passed him on the streets of Buenos Aires who knows how often, my father may have talked to him in the early forties when Angel Malinarich Pinto first arrived in Buenos Aires.

Instead, we have been given his children and their children, a whole tribe of Malinariches, much closer to us than the distant cousins who received us with both alacrity and suspicion in Iquique.

It is around that table in that modest house in San Fernando, talking to Angélica's aunts and uncle, to the half-brother and the half-sisters that her father, Humberto, never met or even knew existed, around that table where her grandfather Angel had so many meals, where her great-grandmother Carmela would reminisce about faraway and forbidden Chile, it is around that table as we swap stories and pass around a gourd of good Argentine herb *mate* and compare eyes and foreheads and hair and skin color and celebrate resemblances and remark differences, it is there that I had thought that perhaps this book should end.

What better conclusion to this voyage full of broken lives than a final image of peace, a coming together of what history had savagely separated, the two sides of Angel Malinarich's family meeting thirty years after his death, the story that started tragically in the barren desert ending joyfully in one of the great hybrid cities of the world.

But I have another debt to pay.

There are other dead men and women who are sending messages from the desert and the past, other families and other migrants who walked the lands that Angélica's grandfather forsook, there are voices I have not yet allowed to have their say.

They are demanding to have the last word.

What did I bring back from the desert?

There were answers in Arica.

My trip had taken me wandering through the avenues and armies of the dead and mostly what I had witnessed was violence, abandonment, betrayal, towns turned into ghosts and ghosts turned into emptiness as their destiny was decided from afar. I had watched what the desert does to those who try to squeeze out every last treasure from its rocks and leave nothing behind, I had seen greed and cruelty unveiled under the stark light, I had seen hope swallowed as if it were a drop of rain in the sand.

But that was not all that the desert showed me. It was not only a territory where the dry cesspool of our humanity was revealed for the eye of the future to see, its inhabitants stripped naked of any pretence of redemption. The same barren land without mercy that makes men compete with each other to the death for scant resources, also demands solidarity if they want to survive, whispers to them to draw closer if they wish to overcome the sun and the infinite stone, tells them to trust one another or die. In the desert, the only way to really escape is with someone else by your side. In an environment so unforgiving and hostile, the best, as well as the worst, of our humanity is heightened and magnified.

And of all the stories of hope and wonder I had seen in the desert, none was more moving than that furtively told to me by the Chinchorro mummies of Arica.

A missive sent to me by the oldest mummies in the world, sent to me from eight thousand years ago, when the inhabitants of the coast of Arica and the twin valleys that meet on that seashore first began preserving their dead. All hunter-gatherers manipulate the body that has died. When something that mysterious and terrifying happened to the community, the end of life of one of its members, that person could not be left alone. The body's position was changed and arranged, eviscerated, painted, burnt, flayed, eaten, but something was always done. Death's enigma required an active relationship. But in the case of the Chinchorro dead, according to the archaeologist Calogero Santoro and the historian Jorge Hidalgo, who guided me through the exhibition at the museum of San Miguel de Azapa and then took me to a refrigerated chamber where hundreds of other mummies and thousands of acrid skulls and bones and skeletons were kept and studied, something entirely new and different occurred, something that was not happening at that point in time in any other place on the planet. The Chinchorros took the manipulated bodies and made them form part of their living community.

San Miguel de Azapa: The warehouse of skulls at the museum

It is a disservice to call them mummies, those corpses secured against the passing of time, given the horror and ugliness that the word arouses today, degraded by Hollywood horror flicks and abhorrent evocations of Egyptian tombs. There is no terror, and no bandages or curses spill forth from the fragile clay figures of the Chinchorros, but dignity rather, and beauty and peacefulness. Out of the bodies of the dead, those who survived them carved a different body, made each corpse into a sculptural composition, made art from the skin and the bones and the eyes and the hair, graced each loved one with a death mask.

The mummies were found packed together eight thousand years after their death—not the way in which they are displayed in the glass cases of the museum, but one on top of the other, a man, then a child, then another man, then a woman, then perhaps a dog and another child, a man and once in a while a fetus, buried and then unearthed by the living each time there was another death, the newest member of the community joining the group and adding to it like a real family increases through time, immersed in a collective identity where no individual is set apart from any of the others, no hierarchy can be remarked, no necklace or favorite object or other possession is inhumed with them. The only thing those distant relatives of ours took on their voyage to the other world was their own body. Their own body and one another.

This is the way to respect the dead, I had thought to myself during my brief communion with those mummies on the day my trip to the desert was ending. This is how we should treat one another in life and in death. It was almost, I felt, as if those who were burying the dead were making love to them, caring for them, nursing them in an incubator, preparing them for rebirth, looking after them, revisiting them over and over again. As if they remembered those lives during the days and nights they worked on the motionless bodies, how they connected to each other, remembering the mother who offered milk or the grandfather who had taught the first steps. Re-creating the past in the very action of offering refuge to it with their hands and in the earth. Maybe that was how the Chinchorros wanted to imagine eternity: as a family that cannot be fractured by time or death.

Calogero—who had worked extensively with Lautaro Núñez—explained to me as I looked down onto a darkly radiant child resting not far from the long arms of two adults, that it took several days to make these dead into mummies, a not insignificant expenditure of time and resources. Which means that the moment of death must have been felt as very critical, an emergency for the group. This had to have been an occasion where the long ritual of preparing the dead for conservation reaffirmed the principles and values that sustained that society. There was, of course, no radio, no TV, no print, no alphabet, and these men and women were scattered over three hundred kilometers up and down the coast and into the adjoining oases, and yet, for four thousand years, they kept the same way of honoring the dead, they exhibited an extraordinary sense of group cohesion. The only thing that changed over that lengthy period was that the process became ever more simple, ever more delicate. So death must have been the moment when everyone was gathered around, when the story of the group and the history of the group was dreamt over and over again, repeated so it would not be forgotten. Words were woven that reconstituted the group and, in some way we can scarcely envision, must have healed it.

As Calogero spoke, I was transported back to the beginning of my trip three weeks ago, when Mario Pino had summoned forth from the receding tides of thirteen thousand years ago the nights when knowledge had been conveyed from one generation to the next inside the toldos at the encampment in Monte Verde. It was almost as if the two extremes of my voyage were entering into some sort of echoing dialogue, the stories of the Chinchorros while they tended their dead answered by the stories the men and women of Monte Verde told each other to tend to their living, the connection I was establishing made all the more poignant because the one thing that Monte Verde had not revealed to the future was how its residents dealt with their dead. Not one human bone, not one hint at a possible ceremony, not any sense of what death meant to them had been left behind.

When I had planned my journey, I knew nothing about the lack of mortuary customs in that oldest settlement in the Americas near Puerto Montt. I only had the intuition that I needed to begin the trip to the North in that farthest moment in time, and that I had to see—and if not see, feel the weight of—the huella. I was obsessed with carrying the footprint of that child gently imprinted in my brain as I ventured forth into the vast cemetery of the desert. That decision seemed, in retrospect, to have been wise. My journey had started in a place in the South where death had not yet been conceived, where no human remains could be found, and had finished all the way at the other extreme of Chile, to the far North where five thousand years later other natives had faced that death and sung to it and tamed it and perhaps even held the illusion that it could be conquered. A dance that interlaced through my head: the child who had been laid out next to his or her relatives in the dry sands near Arica somehow calling out to the invisible boy or girl who had left that slight trace in the wetness next to the creek in the area of Puerto Montt, that first footstep left intact in the history of the Americas connecting to all the other feet that had walked this continent from the tip of Alaska to the Strait of Magellan.

Footsteps that I also found in Arica, that had yet another message for me from the dead and the desert.

Ever since my trip had begun I had been hoping to catch a glimpse of the pictographs and the rock paintings that the first inhabitants of the Norte Grande and the Norte Chico had spread over the hills and mountains and *quebradas,* figures in stone that still spoke to travelers and intruders and would-be dwellers so many years later. Flocks of llamas and flights of *condores,* totemic lizards and slow guanacos, men radiating authority like the sun and men holding up threatening staffs, an array of symbolic bodies carved into the ravines and dunes from La Serena to Arica or delineated by dark rocks silhouetted against a lighter background, thousands of years of hands pictographing intricate and complex designs onto the face of that desert. That had been one of the sights, I swore to myself, that I had to capture on this trip—and yet I had not been able to descry even one of them. On the last leg of our journey, on that May 25, the final Saturday afternoon when we would be on the road, we had stopped four, maybe five times after we left Pisagua on our way to Arica and, with increasing exasperation, had scanned the towering sides of rolling dragon hills, those long kilometers of sand ramparts cut out of the meseta wastes by millions of years of rivers that never make it to the sea, we had done our best to locate the famous *geoglifos* and *petroglifos.* But our eyes were not like the eyes of the indigenous people who used to trek through these routes, and we had detected nothing, not a picture, not a pattern. It was only to be in Arica, once I was ready to say good-bye to the Chinchorro mummies, that Santoro and Hidalgo would guide me to those figures hewn upon the three-hundred-meter walls that flank the twin green snaking oases of Azapa and Lluta and that had been waiting for me, I thought, ever since I had left Monte Verde three weeks ago.

There were endless theories about why the original inhabitants of this area went to the considerable trouble of scaling the arid slopes and leaving their gigantic artistic mark upon them.

As my friends explained to me as I gazed upward in awe—again, looking toward the sky as I had done on the Cerro Las Campanas to try to press from remote origins some contemporary intimation of meaning—these figures were linked to the routes where traffic and trade used to pass through, they are the guardians of the passageways that connect the sea to the highlands and therefore signal the central incessant nomadic movement that made the desert a place of habitation, shells from the coast appearing up in the Andes, smelting techniques from the mountains being used on the shores of the Pacific. Those figures telling voyagers where they are and how to proceed. But also markers of territory, situated at precisely the point where the valley opens up and widens, placed there to stop strangers from penetrating a territory that already belonged to another tribe, a way of defending the back-and-forth caravan with tutelary gods. *Here we are,* the figures are saying, *don't mess with us, we are powerful, look at what we have carved up here on this mountain, if we could paint these votary bodies up here, think of what we could do to you down there. We are in communication with these spirits.*

I was listening attentively to my guides and their elucidations made all the sense in the world, but what was really haunting me were other thoughts, there, at the end of my journey, at this place where so many journeys had started and ended, so many men and animals had passed through on their way to somewhere else. I was looking up at those enormous *gigantones* with their large square faces and a sort of hood behind their head and something like a knapsack on their back and those vertically rectangular bodies where the trunk was separated from the head and the legs splayed out, and what impressed me most, perhaps because I was looking for it, needing it, wanting to imagine it, was that these figures were extremely dynamic. It was as if they were always about to walk or had been caught in the middle of their journey, one foot on the verge of stepping forward, on the verge of moving or dancing or … The feet that had explored this desert, one step after the other, that had transformed it into a land that humans could inhabit for a while, trying to make believe they were here permanently.

And telling us something else that we had forgotten, that those who came later, searching for silver and gold and guano and copper and nitrate, had not been able to understand.

We have lost the tradition that gave birth to the deepest meaning of those figures up there.

Every voyage is perilous.

And you prepare for it by praying and you end it by being thankful.

That then is what they were telling me as my voyage drew to its conclusion, as my voyage promised other voyages, as this desert told me that there were some lessons it had taught me that I should not allow myself to ignore.

So here is my prayer, my thanks for having completed this journey. My own writing, my own signposts, my own way of marking the road we took, recognizing the lives that were given to us to remember and care for and transmit. I want this book to be a small offering, a *gracias* for having been steered so softly through the ghost reaches of my country, the place where Chile and the family I married into and the world I inhabit, where it all had its origin.

What did I finally bring back from the desert?

Gratitude.

Acknowledgments, Along with a Final Story

A book that ends on a note of gratefulness cannot very well leave unthanked those who made this trip possible, starting of course with Angélica, to whom this book is dedicated and who not only had to suffer through all my hallucinations and detours during the voyage itself but the far worse madness of the writing process.

It goes almost without saying that all of the men and women whose names are mentioned in the preceding pages contributed significantly to our quest in the North. But of what use would it be to list all over again each and every one of them, how they took us into their homes and offices and work-shops, how they showered us with gifts and meals and stories?

I do need, however, to briefly recognize those who helped me in ways that went far beyond the call of duty. The shape of this trip owes much to Sergio Bitar, who spent many hours phoning, helping me hatch plans, and I am only sorry that he was unable to join us in Antofagasta. Nor should I forget the efforts of Natalia Varela, who organized most of my program in Iquique, Pisagua, and Arica. As to Lautaro Núñez, he not only provided the wisdom and camaraderie that are attested to in many chapters of this tome, but also opened many doors in his native Iquique. Nor would Arica have afforded me the wonderful guidance of Calogero Santoro had Lautaro not arranged that particular link with his disciple and collaborator. Mario Pino was particularly gracious before, during, and after my visit to Monte Verde; Carolina Agüero provided us with overwhelming (and much needed) hospitality and intelligence in San Pedro de Atacama; Senén Durán was exceptionally generous with his time and his knowledge; and Ivor Ostoijic and his wife went out of their way to make us feel at home in the city where Angélica's ancestors had disembarked. Thanks also to Pelao Gavilán for the many meals he cooked for us at El Vagón—particularly the last one. And of course Jinny—thank you for allowing me into your life and Freddy's. And Miguel Roth and Jenny under the stars and there's Hernán Rivera Letelier and his wife, Mari, and ... but I am on my way to cataloguing the whole roster, I seem to be breaking my promise to spare readers a prolonged roll call.

Better then that I should now highlight some of those whose names were not mentioned in *Desert Memories* and who nevertheless were crucial to the success of this excursion. Gloria Figueroa and her staff at the Hotel Orly gave us the support and friendliness we have come to expect each time we stay at that extraordinary hotel in Santiago. And Jin Auh, my friend who represents me at the Wylie Agency, offered me invaluable support, both when defining the voyage and over the months it took to finish the manuscript during a time that could not have been easy for her. Jennifer Prather, my assistant, unflinchingly answered my needs for information and juggled schedules and bibliographies with equal measures of goodwill and cheerfulness. And the Duke University library did its habitually competent job in furnishing the books and texts I required to seek out the origins of just about everything on this planet. And I was privileged to have the support and enthusiasm of Elizabeth Newhouse and Larry Porges at National Geographic, with special recognition and indebtedness to my editor, John Paine, who carefully read the manuscript and made it so much better with his intelligent suggestions.

But a pilgrimage such as this one should not end without a final story, a story that is also, in its way, an acknowledgment.

The last night of my journey, the night of Sunday, May 26, 2002, just before I took the plane back to Santiago, I visited Don Fortunato Manzano Manzano at his home in the barrio of San José in Arica.

I had gone to see him because he is a *yatiri,* an Aymara shaman who was born in the highlands of the Andes, very close to where Chile meets Bolivia and Peru, and now spends most of his time in Arica tending to the souls and bodies of the many Indian inhabitants of the city. I had imagined, when first planning the trip, that it would be particularly appropriate to meet, at the very end of my wanderings in the desert, one Chilean who was descended from its original inhabitants, someone who still claimed to be the intermediary between heaven and Earth, the *altiplano* and the sea, the gods above and the gods below. A man whose primary language was not Spanish (and certainly not English), but the Aymara that had been spoken in these lands before the conquistadores came and that had survived all the subsequent invasions and humiliations. I nursed the vague idea that perhaps something might be revealed to me in that encounter, if I placed it at the very end of my voyage.

It turned out that I was unable to spend as much time with Don Fortunato as I would have liked. I got lost in the labyrinth of streets of the barrio made up almost entirely of Aymara Indians, and did not connect with him till several frustrating hours had gone by. Indeed I had begun to wonder, as I roamed and rambled and interrogated neighbors and residents, whether his extremely nebulous instructions on how to find his house had not been a sort of test, a way in which he was determining whether I wished to contact him enough to persevere. But the real reason I could not have a longer conversation with him once I did manage to stumble on his abode was that my body had suffered a back spasm at the very instant the day before when I had finished unloading our bags from the car at our hotel in Arica. My back has given me trouble for years and this was not the first time that, at the end of a prolonged trip—and in this case I had just driven thousands of miles—as soon as my muscles begin to relax, I am racked with pain.

Angélica had requested that I cancel all my Arica engagements and spend our last day on this journey resting with her at the luxuriously verdant Azapa Inn. Hadn't we had enough of dust and roads? Didn't I need to take care of my health? But I left her there, at the very entrance to the oasis stretching many miles into the faraway mountains, enjoying the lush greenery and flowers and hum of birds that would rival any Garden of Eden anywhere, and set out to meet the mummies and the giant figures that I fiercely knew I had to see. So I admired the calm tender immobility of the mummies even if I could not rest myself, I communed with those dynamic gods up on the hills striding into eternity even though I might be limping, keeping my appointment with the first migrants who had happened upon these lands ten thousand years ago.

My ache and paralysis and tiptoe movements making me even more determined as the day wore on, that I should also meet at least one descendant of those migrants, those people who had made this desert their home, I would shake the hand of Don Fortunato Manzano Manzano even if it killed me.

Our meeting was not going to kill me.

We talk about many things with the yatiri, one more exploration of how the culture of the Andes intersects with our contemporary world and sends us messages that we would do well to heed and—and I would love to go on, I really would, but after a while I cannot stand the pain and I rise gingerly from the sofa and tell Don Fortunato that I must unfortunately leave, the day has been far too long, the journey even longer.

"You cannot go," he says, "not before I give you something for your back," and disappears into the arcane rear of the house from where feminine voices have come floating and the echo of a door that opens and closes, opens and closes. And then he reemerges with a potion in his hand, a sort of balm that smells of eucalyptus and other less definable aromas, herbs from the altiplano, the yatiri says, and orders me to lie down on the sofa and undress so my back is exposed to his touch.

I close my eyes.

"Do you believe in Aymara medicine?" his voice asks.

I tell him the truth. Yes and no. I believe and do not believe.

Behind me and above me I hear him mutter words to God and the Virgin in Spanish and after making the cross—I can feel the faint rustle made by the wind of his fingers in the air—he recites something in Aymara, and then deeply applies the salve, burns it briefly into my back, where the pain is most intense. He rubs for not more than a minute. He says this part is very cold and when I tell him that in the States ice is used to soothe a tense muscle, he snorts and commands me to keep the afflicted area as warm as I possibly can and not to wash the oil off.

And it works, his concern for me, that care from a stranger.

It works, not just that evening and the next day. In all the days that followed, I have not had one new incident of back spasm, not even one night or dawn of distress since Don Fortunato Manzano Manzano pressed his fingers into my bones in Arica six months ago.

The last gift from the desert. That I bear in my very body. The balm that an Aymara healer had received from his father, perhaps from his mother, a form of wisdom that had been transmitted down and down from who knows how many generations back and back, back and back to the very limits of human time, a last gift from those men and women and, yes, children, who had first walked America, danced America, loved this land.

They must have known something about easing pain.

They must have known something about defeating death in the desert.

NATIONAL GEOGRAPHIC DIRECTIONS

Featuring works by some of the world's most prominent and highly regarded literary figures, National Geographic Directions captures the spirit of travel and of place for which National Geographic is renowned, bringing fresh perspective and renewed excitement to the art of travel writing.